A Faithful Spirit

Preparing for Chanukah

מְגִלַּת אַנְטִיוֹכוּס

A Study Text Based on the Midrash
M'gillat Antiochus

Edited with commentary by Benjamin Levy

URJ Press
New York, New York

Library of Congress Cataloging-in-Publication Data

Levy, Benjamin, Rabbi.
    A faithful spirit : preparing for Chanukah: a study text based on the midrash
M'gillat Antiochus / edited with commentary by Benjamin Levy – 1st American paperback ed.
        p. cm.
    Includes the text of the Scroll of Antiochus in Hebrew and English.
    Includes bibliographical references and index.
    ISBN-13: 978-0-8074-0933-6 (pbk. : alk. paper)
    ISBN-10: 0-8074-0933-2 (pbk. : alk. paper)
      1. Scroll of Antiochus. 2. Hanukkah. 3. Jews–History–586 B.C.-70
A.D. 4. Maccabees. I. Scroll of Antiochus. English & Hebrew. II. Title.

BS1825.53L48 2007
296.4'35 22

                                                    2007032181

Typesetting: El Ot Ltd., Tel Aviv
Printed on acid-free paper
Copyright © 2008 by Benjamin Levy
Manufactured in the United States of America

10 9 8 7 6 5 4 3 2 1

Not by might, nor by power, but by My spirit alone,
says the Eternal of Hosts.

Zechariah 4:6; *Haftarat Shabbat Chanukah alef*

For

Evelyn, ***Eli***, and ***Reuven***—

Thank you for the *ruach* and the roots.

Contents

Permissions

Acknowledgments

"When the five sons of Mattathias heard, they got up and went to Mitzpah Gilead, where the House of Israel had been saved in the days of Samuel, the prophet. They decreed a fast, and sat on ashes, and sought mercy from before the God of the heavens. Then a good plan 'fell into their heart'" (M'gillat Antiochus 4:43–50, p. 60).

The midrash depicts the Maccabean community of committed Jews alighting to Mitzpah Gilead for what may be termed a "spiritual retreat." There, as a holy community, they engage in prayer and t'shuvah (the object of fasting). That the text alludes to the prophet Samuel's spiritual history in Mitzpah implies more than collective memory, for it must be remembered that it is the Bible that records Samuel's exploits. Therefore, the mention of Samuel in this context points to the Maccabean community growing spiritually by engaging in Torah study.

As for me, the Etz Chaim community that I have served over these past ten years stands as a house of prayer, Torah study, and spiritual growth. In particular I want to recognize the Matmidim (Constant Torah Learners) adult education group for studying the chapters of this book and offering their interpretations, commentaries, and advice. The group includes Amy and Sid Appleman, Allen Bluestein, Lori and Jeff Brown, Marge Estrin, Sally and Stuart Lind, Harriet and Howard Katz, Frank Malchman, Anita Pearl, Stan Perlman, Len Smollen, and Annette Winter ע״ה.

I also wish to thank Rabbis Jonathan Lubliner and Claudio Kogan for asking me to speak to their respective congregations about A Faithful Spirit. Appreciation also goes out to my good friend Cantor Joel Colman for allowing me to address a joint session of all the Reform congregations in New Orleans with some Chanukah insights as addressed in M'gillat Antiochus one scorching Shabbat summer morning.

I wish to express my gratitude to Rabbi Norman Cohen, provost and professor of midrash at Hebrew Union College–Jewish Institute of Religion, and my mentor. From the outset, Rabbi Cohen assured me of the value of this project and provided suggestions and materials necessary to bring the book to a successful denouement, including steering me to the rabbinic thesis of Rabbi Darcy Crystal. I thank Rabbi Crystal for her generosity in allowing me to benefit from her work.

I thank Myra and Rabbi Leon Klenicki for their inspiration in my becoming a rabbi and for their support as very special members of our Etz Chaim community. I thank

Acknowledgments

Rebbetzin and Rabbi Harold Furst for teaching me what it means to lead a committed rabbinical life.

I especially want to acknowledge the help and support and patience of Rabbi Hara Person, editor in chief of the URJ Press. Her guidance and professional expertise have once again proved immeasurably helpful. She penned the title A Faithful Heart and is the force behind A Faithful Spirit. Beyond that, Rabbi Person is a mensch—not only a privilege to work with, but a pleasure to know. I would also like to thank the staff of the URJ Press, especially Debra Hirsch Corman, Ron Ghatan, Victor Ney, Rebecca Baer, Mike Silber, and Chris Aguero.

I would be remiss without mentioning my friends Mark Sohmer, Jack Wertheimer, and Ives Tucker, who have helped me keep my focus on the book. And where would I be without my family? My wife, Evelyn, and sons, Elijah and Reuven, are towers of strength, partners in the spiritual journey, the source of my roots, and great fun around the chanukiyah year after year.

Finally, I am grateful to my Creator, the Source of blessing and life of the universe, for giving me life, sustaining me, and allowing me to reach this special moment.

Rabbi Benjamin Levy
June 4, 2008
Rosh Chodesh Sivan, 5768

INTRODUCTION

The Historical Context of the Chanukah Story

In considering the events that led to the establishment of the festival of Chanukah, one should arguably begin with the conquest of the ancient Near East by Alexander of Macedonia in 332 B.C.E. This invasion proved vital on two counts. First, it brought about the political changes that eventually led to the kingship of Antiochus IV. His capture and desecration of the Temple in Jerusalem and his promulgation of decrees against the practice of Judaism would galvanize the Jews to rebel, retake, purify, and rededicate the Sanctuary. The Jewish world continues to celebrate the anniversary of that rededication as Chanukah. Second, Alexander's conquest paved the way for Hellenism, a blend of Greek culture and Eastern traditions, to sweep the region. The lure of Hellenism would provide the subtext and fuel the conflict between the Jewish people and Antiochus IV.

For many subjugated peoples, Hellenistic culture, with its art, architecture, geometry, science, theater, and philosophy, represented the most developed civilization that they had ever known. The ancient Near Eastern assimilation to Hellenism tore down barriers between peoples and shattered many traditional religious beliefs and practices. To reinforce this trend, Alexander's successors established many Greek-style city-states throughout Asia and Africa. Each *polis*, or city-state, boasted its own governing assembly of citizens, Greek temple, gymnasium, theater, and public buildings and functioned as a "living center of Greek ideas, values, and institutions."[1]

When Alexander died in 323 B.C.E., his generals divided the empire. Seleucus took the region of Mesopotamia, Persia, and Syria, while Ptolemy ruled Egypt as well as the Land of Israel. During the next hundred years while the Ptolemys and Seleucids (rulers in the lines of succession of the original generals) continued to battle back and forth in an effort to gain more territory, the move toward Hellenization across the Near East gained steam, especially among the Jewish upper classes in the Land of Israel.

By the time Antiochus III, the Seleucid king from Syria and ruler of the Asian region of the empire, wrested control of the Land of Israel from the Ptolemys in 200 B.C.E., the cumulative effect of Jewish exposure to Hellenism clearly began to affect the internal life of the Jews. To some, traditional Jewish observances apparently seemed parochial, separatist, old-fashioned, and even embarrassing. I Maccabees reports that some men went so far as to undergo a painful operation in an attempt to reverse their circumcisions so that when they competed nude in the gymnasium, in accordance with Greek custom, they would not be recognized as Jews.

The Hellenized Jewish elite drew close to the Seleucids. Wealthy Jewish tax farmers became part of the ruling class. When Antiochus IV, who assumed the throne in 176 B.C.E., needed funds to execute his plan to conquer Egypt, he turned to the Tobiad family, well-to-do Jewish tax farmers. They would provide the king a substantial payment, but upon three conditions: They demanded that the High Priest, Onias III, be replaced by his Hellenized brother, Jason, who would himself offer a sizable donation to the king's coffers. They sought the honor of establishing a gymnasium and Hellenist school in Jerusalem. They also wanted to create a *polis* within Jerusalem under the king's protection; theirs would be the prerogative of drawing up a list of citizens of the new political entity, all of whom would be exempt from Jewish law.

As the king agreed to their terms, the Hellenizers founded an "Antiochene citizen-community"[2] in Jerusalem, complete with a gymnasium, Hellenistic school, and other institutions serving the newly enrolled male citizens of the *polis*. Under Jason's leadership, the priests increasingly neglected their Temple duties in favor of Greek athletic competitions, which always included sacrificial tributes to the Greek gods. At one point, Jason sent an offering of three hundred drachmas of silver to pay for idolatrous sacrifices at the festival of Heracles at Tyre. But even Jason was not Hellenistic enough for some. After three years, a layman and even more extreme Hellenizer named Menelaus, with the support of the Tobiads and a large bribe to the king, purchased the high priesthood and, of course, continued to push the Hellenistic agenda.

It was not the case, however, that all Jews supported the drive to abandon the covenant of Sinai and assimilate into the Hellenistic world. A great majority of Jews living in the countryside were unhappy with the activities of Jason and Menelaus and their followers. These Jews proudly maintained their Jewish identities and continued to live their lives according to the commandments of the Torah and the traditions of Judaism. Among the observant Jews was a group known as the Chasidim, or Pietists. Because the Chasidim believed that foreign kings acted as instruments of divine anger, they thought themselves prohibited from any active resistance to the activities of Menelaus, Antiochus, and their supporters. They were quite shocked when upon returning from an unsuccessful military foray against Egypt in 169 B.C.E., Antiochus stopped in Jerusalem and sacked the Temple.

Still, the issues of Hellenization versus loyalty to the covenant at Sinai might have remained an internal Jewish cultural affair had it not been for Antiochus's stationing a military garrison at the Temple in 168 B.C.E. (to prevent anyone from challenging Menelaus's authority) and then desecrating the Sanctuary by instituting an idolatrous pagan cult that sacrificed pigs to Zeus and other Greek deities there. In addition, a year later the king enacted decrees prohibiting the observance of Shabbat, Torah study, circumcision, Rosh Chodesh, and kashrut. Eventually, Antiochus condemned to death anyone deemed to have violated the decrees. The Syrian-Greeks also set up local shrines, upon the king's orders, and pressured Jews to make offerings to their gods and eat of the sacrificial (pig) meat. These actions by Antiochus IV, who by now had dubbed himself "Epiphanes," or "god manifest," moved the Jewish majority, under the leadership of Mattathias the priest and his five sons, to take up arms in rebellion against the king and his Hellenizing supporters.

Although many battles continued to take place over the next thirty-four years, the revolt may be thought of as comprising two primary stages. In its initial phase, 167–163 B.C.E., the people fought to gain religious freedom. This phase culminated in the celebration of the Temple's rededication and establishment of Chanukah as an annual festival. Once they had achieved the right to continue living religiously and culturally as Jews, many continued the fight against the Syrian-Greeks in an effort to gain political sovereignty over the Land of Israel.

Bolstered by knowledge of the mountain terrain and expertise in guerilla tactics, and fueled by the firm belief that they had divine approval as God's covenantal partners to take the initiative, Mattathias and his sons defended their rights to observe Torah. Despite being greatly outnumbered in manpower and weaponry, they achieved many victories. They became known as the "Maccabees," which may mean "hammers," testimony to their bravery and heroism for God's cause.

When Mattathias died in 166 B.C.E., his son Y'hudah took over leadership of the revolt. Y'hudah and his brothers fought valiantly for the Jewish right to remain religiously distinct and succeeded in getting the Seleucid authorities to abandon their anti-Jewish decrees and their policies of coercive Hellenization. By 163 B.C.E., the Maccabees took back the Temple in Jerusalem. Quickly, they cleaned and purified the Sanctuary, fixed the doors, replaced the defiled altar, and repaired the breaches made by the Syrian-Greeks. On the twenty-fifth of Kislev, they rededicated the Temple with an eight-day festival of psalms of praise, prayer, and thanksgiving offerings. They resumed all the aspects of priestly service there, including the placing of the bread of display and kindling of the menorah.

They established the eight-day celebration of the Temple's dedication (or Chanukah) as an annual observance. The Jews of Jerusalem sent letters to Diaspora Jewry to urge their acceptance of Chanukah as an annual celebration. The Sages responded, confirming the festival's observance for generations to come.

In the second stage of the rebellion, the Maccabees, having achieved religious liberty, sought political independence. Without a clear-cut religious goal, Y'hudah's armies shrank. In 161 B.C.E., both he and his brother Elazar were killed in battle. Over the next twenty years, Y'hudah's brothers Yonatan and Shimon served as Jewish military and political leaders. They skillfully engaged in the political intrigues characteristic of the various reigning kings and contenders for the Seleucid throne in an effort to gain independence from the Syrian-Greeks. In 142 B.C.E., Shimon finally declared an independent Jewish state. This sovereignty lasted only until 66 B.C.E., when the Roman general Pompeii conquered Jerusalem.

In contrast to the short-lived nature of the period of political independence under the Hasmonean dynasty, the religious freedom won by the Maccabees has endured. Because of their efforts, the Jewish people today not only still exist, but continue to enjoy existence *as Jews.* That is, the Maccabees, in overcoming those internal and external forces pressuring us to assimilate and abandon the Jewish religious enterprise, have protected our ability to live religiously distinct and spiritually rich lives of loyalty to the covenant established at Sinai, to our own day and into the future. It is this spiritual victory that stands as the greatest achievement of Mattathias and his five sons. The ongoing festival of Chanukah symbolizes their accomplishment and continues to speak to us of their prodigious courage and faith, as well as the timeless values of religious freedom and loyalty to the covenant that they championed.

Toward an Understanding of Chanukah: The Role, History, and Structure of the Text

Over the last fifty years, Chanukah has become one of the most popular celebrations among American Jews. The Jewish Population Survey of 2000 indicates that a full 78 percent of American Jews light Chanukah candles.[1] The Festival of Lights has become the most popular time for Jews to exchange gifts. We decorate our homes with signs saying "Happy Chanukah" (or Hanukkah, or Chanuka, or Chanukkah). We feast on potato pancakes and jelly doughnuts, not to mention chocolate gelt. We sing songs written by Peter Yarrow, of Peter, Paul, and Mary fame; and now Adam Sandler, whose song includes the phrase, "Celebrate Chanukah . . . and smoke your marijuanikah." We spin the dreidel, more often than not competing for M&M'S®—now certified kosher, by the way. And yet some venerable and erudite Jewish leaders are uncomfortable. Some say we're making too much out of a "minor festival." Others fear that all this mirth makes "lite" of the Festival of Lights. Or worse, some opine all of this dedication to Chanukah to be externally driven by the holiday's closeness on the calendar to Christmas. There are some like Rabbi Manuel Gold, who argue against the "Christianization" of Chanukah.[2]

This popularization of Chanukah begs us to ask what we might be doing wrong. Is our enthusiasm misplaced? Are we missing something important? What is this Festival of Rededication supposed to be about?

These questions are not new. Addressing the laws of Chanukah, the Talmud (*Shabbat* 21b) poses a now famous enquiry: *Mai Chanukah?* (מַאי חֲנֻכָּה), "What is Chanukah?" This seems a curious question indeed. After all, by the time of the Talmud's redaction, Chanukah had already been celebrated for hundreds of years. In addition, the Rabbis themselves confirmed and established Chanukah as an enduring celebration. Shouldn't they have known what Chanukah was? Why did they need to pose this question?

Explanations of "*Mai Chanukah?*" abound. Some think the Talmud is actually asking: "Why do we say *Hallel* [psalms of praise] on Chanukah?" Others suggest that the question means: "Why does the celebration of this postbiblical festival last for eight days?" Still others interpret the Talmud's enquiry thusly: "Which miracle do we really celebrate through Chanukah: the Maccabean victory over the Syrian-Greek oppressors and their henchmen, or the oil that burned for eight days?" In other words, "What is the origin of this festival?"

The Talmudic enquiry and all of the speculation surrounding it seem to reflect an arrant lack of understanding concerning this Rabbinically ordained festival and the reason for its existence. The Talmud's question has less to do with the origin of Chanukah than discerning what its meaning might be for Jews in Talmudic times and later generations.

When trying to determine the meaning of holidays, we would usually consult the *Tanach* and the siddur. With the other festivals of the Hebrew calendar, biblical citations and distinctive liturgies go a long way to answer questions of meaning. Since Chanukah is postbiblical, it does not have the advantage of specific mention in the Torah[3] or a canonic "scroll" dedicated to it, as is the case with *M'gillat Esther* and the insight it provides into Purim. Liturgically, there is a very short list of prayers exclusively dedicated to Chanukah, the most prominent being the one paragraph *Al HaNisim*, inserted into the *Amidah* and the *Birkat HaMazon* during the festival's eight days.[4]

While there do exist four ancient books known as I Maccabees, II Maccabees, III Maccabees, and IV Maccabees, the Sages purposely excluded them from the biblical canon of the *Tanach*. As such, they have come to be known as a part of a collection commonly called the Apocrypha, or "those books left out."[5] Consequently, the Books of the Maccabees have never become part of the readings or liturgy of the synagogue service and are not viewed as "Jewish" sources on Chanukah.

This dearth of canonic material has thus left something of a gap of Rabbinically authorized resources to use in an effort to better understand and celebrate Chanukah. *M'gillat Antiochus* (also known as *M'gillat Chashmonaim*, "Scroll of the Hasmoneans," and *M'gillat Yavan*, "Scroll of Greece") emerges to fill this gap. This "minor" or short-in-length midrash seeks to address the involved questions of meaning alluded to by the Talmud and to provide a basic understanding of Chanukah's themes. In Italian and Yemenite synagogues, worshipers publicly read *M'gillat Antiochus* each Chanukah, just as Jews the world over read *M'gillat Esther* on Purim. Other Jewish communities have used *M'gillat Antiochus* as a study text to help prepare for and better comprehend Chanukah.

The scroll is first mentioned in *Halachot G'dolot*, the code of law stemming from the early geonic period (seventh century C.E.), as a study text originating in the "oldest schools of Shammai and Hillel." This would place the original publication of *M'gillat Antiochus* sometime in the first century C.E.[6] Most scholars, however, surmise that it was composed during the seventh century C.E. Saadyah Gaon, in his *Sefer Galui*, refers to the scroll as the "Book of the Sons of the Hasmoneans" as he quotes from the text.

In addressing the meanings of Chanukah and expounding upon its themes, the author of *M'gillat Antiochus* has created a cohesive biblical-style narrative that has come down to us in two ancient languages: an Aramaic version, which most scholars agree to have been the original, and a word-for-word Hebrew translation. In composing the narrative, the author weaves together various biblical phrases and motifs, midrashic traditions, historical sources, apocryphal works, and liturgical expressions to depict and in effect comment upon the events that led to the establishment of Chanukah.

Biblical Phrases and Motifs

The author of *M'gillat Antiochus* has composed the midrash using the biblical narrative style. Narrative sections employ the conversive *vav* (which changes the tense of the conjugated verb), while the author represents characters' speech by verbs in their "plain" or simple conjugation. This technique accomplishes more than provide a traditional feel to the piece. It communicates that this Rabbinically ordained festival of Chanukah is actually deeply rooted in the tradition of the Torah, not alien to it.

The style likewise lets us know that the zealotry of the Maccabees is grounded in biblical tradition. Their zeal in defending the Jewish people and Judaism constitutes nothing new or different from that which already appears on the Bible. In fact, the actions of Yochanan in killing the Syrian-Greek general Nikanor echoes a pattern of zealotry already established in the Book of Numbers in the incident of Pinchas versus Cozbi and Zimri (Numbers 25:1–13), and the case of Ehud against Eglon, the Moabite king, as depicted in the Book of Judges (3:13–30).

All of these instances (the Maccabees, Pinchas, and Ehud) exhibit certain common features. First is a sense of exigency, as the continued existence of the Jewish people is clearly threatened. Second, the zealot plays upon the ego of the perpetrator (or perpetrators in the case of Pinchas) to gain the private access necessary to take action. Third, the hero pulls a hidden weapon from beneath his clothing,[7] indicating forethought and daring. Fourth, while involved in executing the act of zealotry, the protagonist mentions God, illustrating a purity of motive as opposed to a personal vendetta.

In addition to being expressed in the style of Scripture, *M'gillat Antiochus* reflects the biblical motif of oppression (specifically, a genocide that threatens the existence of the Jewish people) and redemption. This motif is found operating in chapters 1–20 of the Book of Exodus and again throughout *M'gillat Esther*. The Book of Exodus depicts the Pharaoh, king of Egypt, attempting to wipe out the Jewish people by enslaving them, murdering their male children upon birth, and eventually decreeing that they all be thrown into the river and drowned. But God, working through the human agents of Moses, Aaron, and Miriam, defeats the evil king, who pretends to be a god. Hence, God's people are redeemed, and then God brings them to a place of holiness, Mount Sinai. There the people experience the Divine and receive revelation.

In *M'gillat Antiochus*, we read of an evil king who also threatens to destroy the Jewish people, not by throwing babies into a river, but by outlawing the practice of Judaism. But God, again working through human agents, the Maccabees, defeats Antiochus, who pretends to be a god. Thus God sparks redemption for the Jews and then leads them to a holy place, the Temple in Jerusalem. There God blesses them with reve-lation in the form of a one-day supply of oil that lasts for eight days.

In the story of the Exodus, however, God's redemption is done in the open, easily recognized by all who see it. The Ten Plagues over Egypt and the splitting of the Reed Sea would have been tough to miss by anyone present. The tale of Chanukah as expressed in *M'gillat Antiochus*, however, features a more hidden God. Yes, divine power supports and ensures the Maccabees' victory of the few over the many, the righteous over the arrogant, and the weak over the strong. But God remains hidden throughout the midrash, leaving more room for human initiative than in the Exodus story. In this aspect, *M'gillat Antiochus* parallels *M'gillat Esther*.

M'gillat Esther, like *M'gillat Antiochus*, includes an evil plot that threatens to destroy the Jewish people and features God working "behind the scenes," as it were, while God's human covenantal partners demonstrate the initiative and bravery to set the divine redemption in motion. The two scrolls share other parallels as well. In both, support for a murderous rampage against the Jews is gained by citing Jewish religious distinctiveness. Haman, the villain of *M'gillat Esther*, seeks permission to exterminate the Jews by arguing before the king, "There is a certain people scattered abroad and dispersed among the peoples in all the provinces of your realm. Their laws are dif-ferent from every other people's. And they do not observe the king's laws" (Esther 3:8). In *M'gillat Antiochus*, the king, seeking support from his officers for his designs against the Jews, speaks similarly, "Do you not know that there is this Jewish people among us in Jerusalem? They do not sacrifice to our gods, nor do they observe our religion [laws], and they abandon the king's laws to practice their own" (*M'gillat Antiochus* 1:22–27).

Both pieces also begin with a similar formula. *M'gillat Esther* opens: "It happened in the days of Ahasuerus, the Ahasuerus who reigned from Hodu to Cush, over a hundred and twenty-seven provinces" (Esther 1:1). *M'gillat Antiochus* commences: "It happened in the days of Antiochus, king of Greece: he was a great and powerful king, mighty in his dominion, and all the kings heeded him" (*M'gillat Antiochus* 1:1–4).

Both also end with like results: with the punishment of the evildoers, and the estab-lishment of a new holiday to commemorate what transpired. Both emphasize the boon for posterity resulting from the celebration. Thus we read in *M'gillat Esther*: "The Jews confirmed and accepted upon themselves and their seed and upon all who might join them, to observe these two days without fail in the manner prescribed and at the proper time each year. Therefore, these days should be remembered and celebrated by every single generation, family, province, and city; and these days of Purim should never cease among the Jews, nor shall their remembrance perish from their descendants"

(Esther 9:27–28). *M'gillat Antiochus* concludes with a statement in the same vein: "Therefore, the Children of Israel observed these days in all their dispersion and called them days of feasting and joy, from the twenty-fifth of the month of Kislev, for eight days. And the priests and the Levites and the Sages who were in the Temple established and accepted these days upon themselves, and upon the children of their children forever, that their seed shall never neglect them" (*M'gillat Antiochus* 6:53–63).

These parallel phrases and motifs serve not only to point out the similarities between the midrash and its biblical counterparts, but to bring their differences into sharper focus. In the Book of Exodus, as well as in *M'gillat Esther*, the evil protagonists seek to annihilate the Jews; that is, they mean to physically wipe them off the face of the earth. In the midrash, however, Antiochus sees Judaism as the problem. According to him, there is nothing incorrigible inherent within the Jews themselves. Rather, it is their religious observance that separates them from the rest of the realm and makes them different from other peoples and antagonistic to the Greek way of life. Hence, Judaism the religion, as opposed to the individuals, must be defeated and destroyed.

While the Pharaoh of the Exodus and Haman as depicted in *M'gillat Esther* begrudge our physical existence and seek to exterminate the Jewish people in part or in entirety, Antiochus threatens us spiritually. The Exodus marks our physical emergence as a distinct people or nationality, and Purim commemorates our continued physical survival as an ethnic group in exile. Chanukah, on the other hand, celebrates our continuity as Jews, our right to remain religiously distinct. Chanukah, as depicted in *M'gillat Antiochus*, therefore informs that it is not enough to merely survive, but Jewish survival must serve a higher, godly purpose. Physical, national, and ethnic survivals are not ends in themselves, but only prerequisites for spiritual growth and sacred behaviors. Our distinctive religious observances, as confirmed through the victory of Chanukah, lift us to a higher plane of holiness and inspire us to the deeds of righteousness that *M'gillat Antiochus* and the Rabbis who established Chanukah as an annual observance see as defining the Jews as a people.

Historical Sources and Apocryphal Works

The many parallels between the major historical and apocryphal sources and *M'gillat Antiochus* help us to contextualize and interpret the midrash. As was the case with the biblical expressions and motifs alluded to above, the disparities between the midrashic text and the major historical and apocryphal sources also significantly add to our understanding of *M'gillat Antiochus* and its message of Chanukah's meaning.

The major historical and apocryphal works recognized as comparative materials are those published closest to the events of Chanukah themselves, both geographically and time-wise: Josephus's *Jewish Antiquities*, and I and II Maccabees. Of these, I Maccabees is probably the most ancient. Jonathan A. Goldstein opines it to have been written sometime around the year 90 B.C.E. as "propaganda to justify the dynastic claims of Alexander Janneus" (of the Hasmonean House, 103–76 B.C.E.).[8] Goldstein dates II Maccabees to circa 76 B.C.E.,[9] and posits it an attempted "refutation of the dynastic propaganda"[10] of I Maccabees. Josephus Flavius (38–100 C.E.) published his *Jewish Antiquities* sometime in the late first century C.E. In it the historian sought to explain to a general audience why the Jews and the Romans had so much trouble getting along.[11] All three of these sources originated in the Land of Israel.

M'gillat Antiochus and the three source texts all share what may be considered the basic "signposts" of the Chanukah story. For instance, all mention certain basic players of the Chanukah drama: Antiochus IV, Nikanor, Bagris, Mattathias, and his five sons. All emphasize the role of the Maccabean victories over the Syrian-Greeks in the establishment of Chanukah (as opposed to the miracle of the oil). Both I Maccabees and *M'gillat Antiochus* mention the fact that the king's armies not only greatly outnumbered the Jewish forces, but also possessed great technological advantage, including elephants.[12] All the texts speak of the desecration of the Temple in Jerusalem, the king's decree against the practice of Judaism, and the martyrdom of those who dared defy the king. Both I and II Maccabees and the midrash include the story of the king's forces martyring the Pietists who have retreated into a cave to observe the Sabbath.[13] *M'gillat Antiochus*, I Maccabees, and Josephus all allude to a Maccabean interlude in Mitzpah between battles. All of the texts include the rededication of the Temple and reestablishment of the priestly service there.

While the parallels between *M'gillat Antiochus* and the historical sources firmly place the midrash within the rubric of "Chanukah literature," the disparities between the scroll and the aforementioned sources bring the distinctiveness of the midrash's message into sharp focus. The disparities begin with the midrash's first chapter when the text mentions Antiochus's intention to "go up against Jerusalem" in the "twenty-third year of his reign" (1:17–21). The historical sources indicate as common knowledge that Antiochus ruled for only eleven years in total. Hence, the midrash from the start reveals its intention to function as an ahistiorical document, far more interested in relating religious truth than historical facts, figures, or accuracy. In functioning as such, *M'gillat Antiochus* reflects its identity as midrashic literature. The term "midrash" means "that which is drawn out." That is, the purpose of midrash is to draw meaning from and interpret events, rather than to provide every historical detail, as would a secular history book. In fact, midrashic literature frequently condenses historical details so that it may better and more clearly concentrate upon the religious significance of the events it relates. Such is the case with *M'gillat Antiochus*.

The religious nature of the midrash's outlook is again evidenced by the condensed version of the Maccabean battles that appears there. While the historical sources report several battles between the Maccabees and the Syrian-Greek forces, *M'gillat Antiochus* includes only three. Moreover, the midrash attributes all the battles to the first phase of the rebellion, the fight for religious freedom. The midrash completely ignores the second part of the uprising, the quest for political sovereignty. The text even places incidents historically belonging in the uprising's second phase, like the death of Y'hudah and the defeat of Nikanor, firmly within the context of the rebellion's first phase, the fight for religious freedom. This emphasis guides one to interpret Chanukah as purely a celebration of religious significance, not a military or political holiday.

The religious purpose of *M'gillat Antiochus* can be discerned in its being the only source to feature the leadership of Yochanan, mostly associating the title "Maccabee" with him, as opposed to Y'hudah. The midrash depicts Y'hudah dying before Jerusalem is won. (This conflicts with the historical sources that report Y'hudah to have championed the first phase of the rebellion and then dying in the battle for political sovereignty that followed.) Why Yochanan? Perhaps, because he is the only brother, except for Elazar (who dies in battle), never associated with political leadership. In fact, the midrash refers to him as the "High Priest of the Jews" (2:19). Even when he acts militarily, the text emphasizes that he does not relish the role. He displays none of the calumny usually associated with military heroes. Rather, he acts with humility as God's servant to do what the Jewish people need in order to survive.

M'gillat Antiochus also differs from II Maccabees in its attitude toward martyrdom. II Maccabees lavishly praises the courage and faith of those whose resistance to Antiochus's anti-Jewish decrees takes the form of allowing themselves to be killed by the Syrian-Greeks for their observance of Judaism. In particular, II Maccabees lauds the Pietists who go to a cave to observe Shabbat and are slaughtered when they refuse to defend themselves on the holy day. *M'gillat Antiochus*, on the other hand, draws a distinction between the attitudes and theology of the Pietists and those of the Maccabees. The midrash praises the Maccabees, who take action against evil, as opposed to the passivity of the Pietists. In addition, the text recognizes the Maccabees as theological innovators. It was the Maccabees who delineated a hierarchy of mitzvot in their ruling that saving one's life outweighs the observance of Shabbat, a priority that came to be institutionalized by the Rabbis. According to the midrash, the Maccabees act as the Rabbis in that they embrace the canonized revelation, yet creatively apply it to the exigencies of their own times.

Liturgical Expressions

M'gillat Antiochus also functions to help one prepare for Chanukah by echoing various liturgical expressions and themes associated with the Festival of Lights. The two most prominent rubrics of prayer specifically attached to Chanukah are *Al HaNisim* and *Hallel*.

The flow of *M'gillat Antiochus* parallels that of *Al HaNisim* ("For the Miracles," added to the *Amidah* and *Birkat HaMazon* throughout Chanukah). Both pieces begin by presenting a powerful "Greek kingdom" that threatens to eradicate Judaism. The Syrian-Greeks outnumber the Jews and exceed them in terms of military strength. At the outset, the Jews, in effect, stand alone while many (a broad coalition of peoples) seek their destruction. But the Jews do not give up. By actively combating the "Greeks," they effect divine assistance to bring about the victory of the weak over the strong, the righteous over the wicked, the observers of Torah over arrogant idolators. Toward the end of the midrash, all those who had joined with Antiochus to oppress the Jews and stamp out Judaism now hound the king, forcing him to become a fugitive. He eventually commits suicide. Both *M'gillat Antiochus* and *Al HaNisim* culminate in the purification of the Sanctuary and the reconstitution of the priestly service there, as symbolized by the kindling of the menorah and the establishment of the eight days of Chanukah as an annual service to God.

Hallel, "Praise," consists of Psalms 113–118 and is traditionally chanted as part of the liturgy for the biblical Pilgrimage Festivals, and on Rosh Chodesh. The fact that Chanukah stands out as the only postbiblical celebration to include the recitation of *Hallel* may be considered an indication of the special nature and stature of the Festival of Dedication. Many sections of *M'gillat Antiochus* echo the liturgical moments of these psalms.

For instance, Psalm 115:1 implores: "Not for our sake, O Eternal, not for our sake, but for Your Name's sake give glory." Expressed in this psalm is the idea that the worshipers pray for redemption, not out of their certainty of their merits, but out of concern for God's reputation and influence on earth. In chapter 2 of *M'gillat Antiochus*, Yochanan beseeches God for deliverance as he is about to go up against Nikanor: "Please do not give me over to this uncircumcised heathen. For if he kills me, he will go and worship in the temple of Dagon his god and say, 'My god gave him over to my hand'" (2:52–56). Echoing the liturgical moment, Yochanan recognizes that he cannot rely upon the strength of his own merits to ensure the success of his mission. Rather, he prays for the sake of God's glory. Thus, Yochanan illustrates not only his humility, but also the purity of his motives, as his intention is to expand divine power and reverence here on earth.[14]

Another example of the connection between Psalm 115 and *M'gillat Antiochus* may be found in the psalm's description of idols: "They have...eyes, but cannot see. They have ears, but cannot hear.... Those who make them, all who trust in them, will become like them"(Psalm 115:5–8). In the midrash, the Syrian-Greeks are blind to the reality that their defeats at the hands of the much smaller and ill-equipped Maccabee forces is actually the result of divine intervention. The Jews full well understand the boon of divine power. As they prepare for the Syrian-Greeks' next inevitable attack, they go to the spiritual center at Mitzpah to pray, repent, and connect with God. This action again echoes the liturgy of Psalm 115, which exhorts: "Israel trust in the Eternal! God is their help and their shield"(v. 9).

In addition, as in *Al HaNisim*, the general flow of the midrash echoes the arrangement of Psalms 116 and 118 of *Hallel*. Psalm 116 speaks of the "pains of death" encircling (v. 3), and Psalm 118 alludes to the "straits" as "all of the nations surround me; in the name of the Eternal I shall cut them down!"(vv. 5, 10). Both psalms culminate in the impulse to thank and praise God for deliverance, "I shall live to relate the deeds of the Eternal" (Psalm 118:17), specifically, to worship God in the Temple, "in the presence of all God's people, in the courts of the Eternal's house, in the midst of Jerusalem. Praise the Eternal!"(Psalm 116:18).

In the beginning of *M'gillat Antiochus*, the Jews find themselves "in the straits" with the "pains of death" encircling, as Israel stands alone against all of the nations led by Antiochus. Then the Jews, however, trusting in the Eternal, take action in God's name. With God as their shield and their help, they are able to cut down their enemies. The midrash culminates, as does *Hallel*, with pilgrimage to the Temple in Jerusalem to praise and worship God in thanksgiving, and with the establishment of the festival of Chanukah to commemorate, publicize, and celebrate the miracle of Jewish spiritual continuity.

These parallels between *M'gillat Antiochus*, *Al HaNisim*, and *Hallel* are important for a few reasons. They tie *M'gillat Antiochus* to the liturgical moments of Chanukah and provide a deeper context for those moments, hence enriching the celebration of Chanukah. In addition, the parallels between the Book of Psalms and the midrash firmly place this postbiblical holiday within the framework of those festivals commanded in the Torah. This not only raises the status of Chanukah, but confirms the authority of the Rabbis to interpret Torah and establish community norms for the Jewish people. It also provides one answer to the question of why Chanukah is the only postbiblical holiday during which *Hallel* is recited.

Themes and Structure of the Text

The midrash opens with King Antiochus's violent and furious campaign to stamp out Judaism and establish a Hellenistic homogeneity in the land of Judea and throughout the ancient Near East. The Jews exhibit three disparate responses to this challenge. Some enthusiastically assimilate into Greek culture and religion, thus abandoning the covenant established at Sinai. Others adopt a policy of passive piety so rigid that they welcome martyrdom rather than defend themselves on the Sabbath. The third faction, led by the Hasmoneans (Mattathias and his five sons, also dubbed the Maccabees), zealously defends the people's right to religious freedom against the king's plan to abrogate the covenant while at the same time championing the flexible approach to religious law necessary to save Judaism and the Jewish people.

Three pitted battles ensue between the Hasmonean heroes and enemies of Judaism. The midrash culminates in the aftermath of the Maccabean victories. That is, upon securing the holy city of Jerusalem, the victors purify the Temple, for Antiochus and his henchmen had desecrated God's Sanctuary by practicing idolatrous rites there. As a gesture of faith and religious continuity, the Hasmoneans kindle the Temple's menorah. The one-day supply of pure olive oil utilized for the lights "blessedly" lasts eight days. The Maccabees then establish these eight days, from the twenty-fifth of Kislev each year, as "days of feasting and rejoicing like the days of the Festivals that are written in the Torah" (6:34–36). Thus, the midrash concludes not only on a note of spiritual redemption, but with the assurance that God values and welcomes human initiative. Our continued partnership with the Eternal ensures a sacred relationship that stretches into the future.

The text of the midrash has been divided into six study units. Each study unit or chapter highlights another Chanukah theme elucidated by the midrash. The themes are expressed as dialectic, a contest between conflicting values: terror versus freedom; zeal versus passivity; creativity versus rigidity; earthly (tyrannical) power versus divine omnipotence; continuity versus assimilation; and tradition versus innovation.

A short essay introduces each chapter cueing the reader to the import of the coming material. A running commentary both clarifies the midrash and challenges the reader. The word *p'shat*, a Hebrew term indicating the "simple" or "straightforward," introduces basic, clarifying comments. Commentary labeled *d'rash*, "that which is drawn out," challenges the reader to identify thematic and formulaic parallels, not only in biblical and Rabbinic literature, but in the reader's own life. Thus, the *d'rash* commentary seeks to raise the text in a way that will communicate current relevance and apply the material to the greater questions of life. Explanatory essays and illuminating gleanings follow each of the six study units.

This volume then proves didactic to the reader on several levels. It serves as an example of and fine introduction to Rabbinic literature in general and to the narrative midrashic process specifically. It functions to interpret the events of Chanukah and place them into biblical, historical, and religious frameworks that will add to the reader's understanding and appreciation of the Festival of Lights. But more than that, this book will hopefully provide the reader with the knowledge and inspiration necessary to apply the lessons of Chanukah to his or her life. In this way, *A Faithful Spirit* sees as its ultimate goal the spiritual expansion and religious fulfillment that enhance all of our lives.

M'gillat Antiochus

Chapter 1

Terror versus Freedom: Antiochus Presses Hegemony

The midrash opens by presenting a world yet unredeemed. King Antiochus IV has declared himself a god and actively seeks to consolidate his power by Hellenizing (imposing Greek religion, culture, and political structure upon) the entire ancient Near East through a campaign of terror. Antiochus proves particularly intolerant of Jews, Judaism, and the religious freedom and promise for redemption they represent. As such, he attempts to put an end to the Jewish people through the violent repression of those observances he deems most essential to the maintenance of the covenant established at Sinai. In particular, he proclaims that the practices of Sabbath, New Moon, and circumcision will be punishable by death.

The first chapter of *M'gillat Antiochus* sets the stage for the series of struggles that will culminate in the redemption marked by the establishment of Chanukah, the festival of religious freedom and the light of Jewish identity. These confrontations will pit the allure and strong-armed tactics of Hellenism against the venerable traditions of Judaism. The Maccabees and their comparatively small band of loyal Jews will challenge the mighty armies of Antiochus for the right to determine, with God's help, their destinies as people of faith and conscience. The scions of Sinai will stand up against the corps of intolerance.

On another level, the midrash depicts the effects of earthly tyrannical power versus divine omnipotence. God's will, in this case, is wrought through human initiative and courageous effort of those loyal to that will. In the words of the Chanukah prayer, *Al HaNisim* (For the Miracles), "Through the power of Your spirit the weak defeated the strong, the few prevailed over the many, and the righteous were triumphant."[1]

The situation presented in this chapter serves as more than just an epic depiction of ancient Near Eastern events. Rather, the midrash uses these events as a metaphor for the cultural challenges and bias that we have faced throughout many ages, up to and including our own time. The anti-Semitic statements and attitudes voiced by

Antiochus have a familiar ring to them today, because they are only too current. The cultural challenges of living within a dominant culture that encourages assimilation and sometimes even militates against the distinctiveness of Jewish identity may also prove descriptive of the pressures many modern Jews feel. In the post-9/11 world, the scourge of state-sponsored terrorism as a tool of politico-social change and religious antagonism has become a reality in our daily lives. The rise of Antiochus and the methods he employs are not one-time happenings, but have many parallels throughout the ages, even our own.

1:1	It happened in the days of Antiochus,	וַיְהִי בִּימֵי אַנְטִיוֹכוֹס
1:2	king of Greece:	מֶלֶךְ יָוָן,
	he was a great and powerful king,	מֶלֶךְ גָּדוֹל וְחָזָק הָיָה
1:3	mighty in his dominion,	וְתַקִּיף בְּמֶמְשַׁלְתּוֹ,
	and all the kings	וְכָל הַמְּלָכִים
1:4	heeded him. He conquered many states	יִשְׁמְעוּ לוֹ. הוּא כָּבַשׁ מְדִינוֹת
1:5	and strong kings, and destroyed	רַבּוֹת וּמְלָכִים חֲזָקִים, וְהֶחֱרִיב
1:6	their castles, and burned their temples,	טִירוֹתָם, וְהֵיכְלֵיהֶם שָׂרַף בָּאֵשׁ,
1:7	and imprisoned their people.	וְאַנְשֵׁיהֶם בְּבֵית הָאֲסוּרִים אָסָר.
1:8	From the days of King Alexander there had	מִימֵי אַלֶכְּסַנְדְּרוֹס הַמֶּלֶךְ
1:9	not arisen a king	לֹא קָם מֶלֶךְ
1:10	like him in the entire region beyond the river.	כָּמוֹהוּ בְּכָל עֵבֶר הַנָּהָר.
1:11	He built a great province	הוּא בָּנָה מְדִינָה גְדוֹלָה
	on the seacoast to be	עַל חוֹף הַיָּם לִהְיוֹת לוֹ
1:12	his capital,	לְבֵית מַלְכוּת,
	and he called it the Province of	וַיִּקְרָא לָהּ מְדִינַת
1:13	Antioch after his name.	אַנְטִיוֹכוֹס עַל שְׁמוֹ.
	Also Bagris his second-in-command	וְגַם בַּגְרִיס מִשְׁנֵהוּ
1:14	built another province	בָּנָה מְדִינָה
	opposite it,	אַחֶרֶת לְנֶגְדָּהּ,
1:15	and he called it	וַיִּקְרָא לָהּ
	the Province of Bagris after his	מְדִינַת בַּגְרִיס עַל
1:16	own name, and such are their names	שְׁמוֹ, וְכֵן שְׁמוֹתָן
	still today.	עַד הַיּוֹם הַזֶּה.

P'shat: **1:1. It happened in the days.** This is a common biblical phrase identifying the historical timeframe of the midrash's action and establishing it as a biblical-style narrative. **1:1. Antiochus.** Antiochus IV, who dubbed himself Epiphanes, or "god manifest." Of the Seleucid dynasty that ruled after the death of Alexander the Great, Antiochus IV reigned over the areas of Mesopotamia, Syria, and Judea from 175 to 164 B.C.E. **1:2. king of Greece.** Antiochus proved to be an avid promoter of Greek culture and religion, otherwise known as Hellenism. He did not rule over the geographic area of Greece. **1:3–4. all the kings heeded him.** Antiochus had already achieved political and territorial conquest, but this was obviously not enough to satisfy his lust for power. **1:6. burned their temples.** According to Rabbi Norman Cohen, the Hebrew הֵיכָלִים (*heichalim*) refers to religious places of power.[2] Thus, we may understand that Antiochus used his campaign of terror to destroy the religions of others. **1:8. King Alexander.** Known as Alexander the Great (356–323 B.C.E.), he emerged from Macedonia to conquer the entire ancient Near East, including Syria, Persia, and Egypt. Alexander was the first to introduce Greek culture to the land of Judea. **1:9–10. a king like him.** Antiochus may have been comparable to Alexander as related to the degree of his power. However, Alexander remained comparatively respectful of the various faiths and religious adherents who populated his empire. According to Josephus (*Antiquities* 11.8), Alexander canceled Jewish taxes during the Sabbatical years and even sent animals to be sacrificed on his behalf in the Temple in Jerusalem. Antiochus, on the other hand, dedicated himself to violent intolerance, particularly when it came to the Jews. **1:10. beyond the river.** On the east side of the Euphrates, the region of Syria and Mesopotamia. **1:11. seacoast.** The area settled by the Philistines, enemies of the Jewish people, as we read in Judges 16:21 regarding the Israelite hero Samson. **1:13. Antioch.** Also the name of his capital city in Syria. **1:15–16. after his own name.** A sign of hubris.

D'rash: **1:1. It happened.** The Hebrew וַיְהִי (*va-y'hi*) is a grammatical form that makes use of the conversive *vav* (the *vav* that changes the tense of the verb). This is a typical feature of biblical narrative. Thus, the midrash establishes at the outset a connection between itself and Holy Scripture, a chain of continuity linking those holidays revealed in the Torah with the postbiblical festival of Chanukah. **1:1. It happened in the days of Antiochus.** The very beginning of the midrash echoes that of the Scroll of Esther, "It happened in the days of Ahasuerus." Just as the Scroll of Esther features the Jewish people taking initiative against a corrupt government plot to exterminate them because of their religious differences, so too does *M'gillat Antiochus* relate the story of the Jewish people taking action against their governmental oppressors. In both

5

instances, the text portrays the miracle of Jewish survival in what might be termed a "hidden" manner. That is, God seems to work "behind the scenes" through human agency, as opposed to openly revealing the divine plan and power, as was the case with the Exodus from Egypt. See also Genesis 14:1, "It happened in the days of Amraphel, king of Shinar," where the Torah utilizes this same phrase to introduce the "war of the four kings against the five" and Abraham's expedition to recover his captured nephew, Lot. **1:2. king of Greece.** According to scholar Victor Tcherikover, "In the Hellenistic period the term 'Greek' ceased to be a purely ethnic [one], and became also a cultural concept. The Greeks did not always make a distinction between a Greek who had come from Greece to settle in oriental lands, and an Oriental who had learned Greek and acquired Greek culture."[3] **1:8. King Alexander.** Opening the midrash with mention of Alexander, the man who introduced Hellenism to the ancient Near East, immediately helps define the issue of the maintenance of Jewish identity versus assimilation into the majority culture as one that will run throughout the piece. **1:13. Antioch.** Some commentators understand the report of II Maccabees 4:9 that Jason, the corrupt and Hellenizing High Priest, desired to build a gymnasium "and to enroll the people of Jerusalem as citizens of Antioch" to indicate the intention on the part of the assimilationists to make Jerusalem a Greek-style *polis* named Antioch. Alternately, the phrase might mean that Hellenized Jerusalemites would be honorary citizens of the capital city Antioch, in Syria. II Maccabees 4:19 records the "Antiochian citizens from Jerusalem" as envoys of Jason, bringing three hundred silver drachmas as a sacrifice to the god Hercules, on the occasion of the quadrennial games in Tyre. **1:13. Bagris.** Although this name does not appear as such in the Books of the Maccabees or Josephus, Rabbi Darcy Crystal points out that the minor midrashim *Maaseh Chanukah* and *Maaseh Chanukah, Nusach Bet* do mention Bagris as "playing a major role." I Maccabees 7:8 and Josephus's *Antiquities* 12:10–11 do mention a Bacchides as a "Friend of the King" and a general of Antiochus, respectively. Therefore, Crystal surmises Bagris to be a Hebraization of Bacchides.[4]

1:17	In the twenty-third year of his reign,	בִּשְׁנַת עֶשְׂרִים וְשָׁלֹשׁ שָׁנִים לְמָלְכוֹ,
1:18	this was the two hundred and	הִיא שְׁנַת מָאתַיִם
1:19	thirteenth year since the erection of the	וּשְׁלֹשׁ עֶשְׂרֵה לְבִנְיַן
1:20	House of God, he determined to go up	בֵּית הָאֱלֹהִים, שָׂם פָּנָיו
1:21	against Jerusalem. He spoke up to his	לַעֲלוֹת לִירוּשָׁלָיִם. וַיַּעַן
1:22	officers, saying, "Do you not know that	וַיֹּאמֶר לְשָׂרָיו: "הֲלֹא יְדַעְתֶּם כִּי
1:23	there is this Jewish people among	יֵשׁ עַם הַיְּהוּדִים אֲשֶׁר
1:24	us in Jerusalem? They do not	בִּירוּשָׁלַיִם בֵּינֵינוּ. לֵאלֹהֵינוּ אֵינָם
1:25	sacrifice to our gods, nor do they	מַקְרִיבִים, וְדָתֵינוּ אֵינָם
1:26	observe our religion, and they abandon	עוֹשִׂים, וְדָתֵי הַמֶּלֶךְ
1:27	the king's laws to practice their own.	הֵם עוֹזְבִים לַעֲשׂוֹת דָּתָם.

P'shat: **1:19–20. erection of the House of God.** That is, the building of the Second Temple. Since its initial construction spanned the years 538–515 B.C.E., and according to most scholars Antiochus did not reign until 175 B.C.E., the midrash may be referring to a specific rebuilding of the Second Temple. On the other hand, the midrash may be communicating something of its primary purpose, in that issues of historical accuracy are less a focal point than the revelation of religious truth. The text's allusion to the twenty-third year of Antiochus's reign, when most historians would count his years in power as only eleven, would further reinforce this notion. **1:24–25. They do not sacrifice to our gods, nor do they observe our religion.** The mention of gods and religion clearly delineates the battle for the Jews as one fought for the right to remain religiously distinctive, to maintain their own culture and covenant in the face of Hellenistic hegemony and social prejudice on the part of the Syrian-Greeks.

D'rash: **1:20–21. go up against Jerusalem.** The Hebrew phrase לַעֲלוֹת לִירוּשָׁלָיִם (*laalot lirushalayim*) can also mean to "go up to Jerusalem" on religious pilgrimage. The phrase points not only to the geographic altitude of the holy city, but the spiritual elevation achieved in making pilgrimage there to observe God's festivals. Therefore, the use of this term vis-à-vis Antiochus proves ironic, for he understands neither the beauty of nor sacredness that may be achieved through Judaism. **1:23–24. there is this Jewish people among us.** This echoes the speech Haman makes to King Ahasuerus (Esther 3:8): "There is a certain people ... in all the provinces of your realm. Their laws are different from every other people's. And they do not observe the king's laws; therefore it is not befitting the king to tolerate them." The Talmud interprets Haman's overture to Ahasuerus to really mean: "They do not eat our food, nor intermarry with us. They waste the whole year [avoiding the king's work] with the excuse, 'Today is Shabbat, today is Pesach'" (*M'gillah* 13b). Thus in both *M'gillat Esther* and *M'gillat Antiochus*, the villain uses the Jewish right to distinctive religious practice as an excuse for their destruction.

1:28	And moreover, they hope for the day	וְגַם הֵם מְיַחֲלִים לְיוֹם
1:29	when the kings and the rulers will be	שִׁבְרוֹן הַמְּלָכִים
1:30	broken, and they are saying,	וְהַשִּׁלְטוֹנִים, וְאוֹמְרִים:
1:31	'When will our king rule over us, and	'מָתַי יִמְלֹךְ עָלֵינוּ מַלְכֵּנוּ,
1:32	then we will have control over the sea	וְנִשְׁלֹט בַּיָּם
1:33	and dry land, so that the entire world	וּבַיַּבָּשָׁה, וְכָל הָעוֹלָם
1:34	will be given into our hand.'	יִנָּתֵן בְּיָדֵנוּ.'
1:35	It is no honor for the kingdom to	אֵין כָּבוֹד לַמַּלְכוּת
1:36	allow them to remain on	לְהַנִּיחַ אֵלֶּה עַל
1:37	the face of the earth.	פְּנֵי הָאֲדָמָה.
1:38	Now, come and we will go up against them	עַתָּה, בּוֹאוּ וְנַעֲלֶה עֲלֵיהֶם
1:39	and we will nullify the covenant	וּנְבַטֵּל מֵהֶם אֶת הַבְּרִית
1:40	their God made with them: Sabbath, New	אֲשֶׁר כָּרַת לָהֶם אֱלֹהֵיהֶם: שַׁבָּת, רֹאשׁ
1:41	Moon, and circumcision."	חֹדֶשׁ וּמִילָה."
1:42	And the thing was good	וַיִּיטַב הַדָּבָר
1:43	in the eyes of his officers and	בְּעֵינֵי שָׂרָיו
1:44	in the eyes of all his army.	וּבְעֵינֵי כָל חֵילוֹ.

P'shat: 1:28. they hope for the day. Antiochus misinterprets the age-old Jewish hope for a messianic age when peace and fraternity will reign. He assumes the messianic prayer to be a plan for world domination and the exploitation of others. Or perhaps he merely uses this argument as a ruse to convince others to join in his quest to persecute the Jewish people. **1:39. nullify the covenant.** Antiochus's goal is not simply political domination. Rather, he is initiating a "religious war" against the Jews and in the process placing himself above divine law by attempting to do away with God's covenant established at Sinai. He has, after all, declared himself a god. **1:40–41. Sabbath, New Moon, and circumcision.** Antiochus deems that doing away with these three observances would be the key to eradicating Jewish identity.

1:40–41. New Moon. Known in Hebrew as רֹאשׁ חֹדֶשׁ (*Rosh Chodesh*), "Head of the Month," the Jewish people in ancient days celebrated the appearance of the new moon. This event, which marked the beginning of a new month on the lunar calendar, was considered a semi-holiday. The Jews brought special sacrifices to the Temple in Jerusalem in honor of Rosh Chodesh. It should be noted that the halachic definition of new moon differs slightly from that of the standard English dictionary. The dictionary refers to that period when no trace of the moon may be seen as the "new moon." The Jewish concept, on the other hand, denotes the first visible sliver of the moon following its cyclic fading from view. **1:43. in the eyes of his officers.** All of Antiochus's officers and army want to eliminate the Jews and stamp out Judaism. They understand the task before them and proceed with open eyes. Antiochus's military actively participate and even take part in the planning. They are not merely following orders.

D'rash: **1:33. the entire world.** A supposed plan for world domination has been a frequent rallying cry throughout the history of anti-Semitism. In modern times, Antiochus's argument for a Jewish conspiracy is documented by a fraudulent book, *The Protocols of the Learned Elders of Zion*, referred to by the Anti-Defamation League as "the most famous and vicious forgery of modern times."[5] The document allegedly consists of the minutes of a secret meeting of a group called the Learned Elders held as part of the First Zionist Congress in Basel, Switzerland, in 1897. The book presents twenty-four protocols, or means, by which the Jews will take over the world, including subverting the morals of the gentiles; controlling the world's gold supply, economies, and banks; and establishing a world regime under a despotic Jewish king. Originally published in abbreviated form in 1903 in the Russian-language newspaper *Znamia* (The Banner), the *Protocols* has appeared in many languages and under many titles over the years. In 1922, Henry Ford distributed tens of millions of copies throughout the United States, under the title *The International Jew*. During the 1930s, Hitler and his Nazi party freely disseminated the document in an effort to rally support for their anti-Semitic policies and, later, to blame the Jews as the true instigators of World War II. In the 1960s, Egyptian president Gamal Abdel Nasser published an Arabic version of the *Protocols* in Egypt. King Faisal of Saudi Arabia began distributing this version during the 1970s. Today, this fraud remains persistently available in every Muslim capital across the Middle East. **1:39–40. the covenant God made with them.** The verb כָּרַת (*karat*) literally means "cut," as covenants in ancient days were thought of being carved in stone. The tablets of the Ten Statements of Exodus, chapter 20, constitute a case in point. Covenants etched in stone are not easily

9

erased. **1:40–41. Sabbath, New Moon, and circumcision.** According to I Maccabees 1:41–57, the royal decree also included a prohibition against offering sacrifice in the Temple (this went into effect the twenty-fifth of Kislev, the date of the Temple's rededication and, hence, the date that would come to be celebrated as the first day of Chanukah), maintaining religious dietary laws (כַּשְׁרוּת, *kashrut*), and Torah study. **1:40. Sabbath.** In the opinion of Rabbi Leo Baeck, ''There is no Judaism without the Sabbath.''[6] The fact that secular Zionist Ahad HaAm wrote, ''More than Israel has kept the Sabbath, has the Sabbath kept Israel,'' again speaks to its essential nature in the scheme of Jewish continuity.[7] **1:41. circumcision.** The mark of circumcision has long been a feature of Jewish identification. According to Rashi, who bases his reading on *B'reishit Rabbah* 93:8, one of the ways that Joseph proves his identity to his brothers after twenty-two years of absence is by drawing them near to him so that they may bear witness to his circumcision: ''Come close to me, if you please'' (Rashi on Genesis 45:4). Even the philosopher Baruch Spinoza reckoned that circumcision ''alone would preserve the nation.''[8]

1:45 Immediately	בְּאוֹתָהּ שָׁעָה
King Antiochus got up and	קָם אַנְטִיוֹכוֹס הַמֶּלֶךְ
1:46 sent Nikanor, his viceroy,	וַיִּשְׁלַח אֶת נִיקָנוֹר מִשְׁנֵהוּ
with a great army	בְּחַיִל גָּדוֹל
1:47 and many people, and	וְעַם רָב,
1:48 he came to the city of Judah,	וַיָּבוֹא לְעִיר יְהוּדָה,
1:49 to Jerusalem,	לִירוּשָׁלַיִם,
and committed a great massacre.	וַיַּהֲרוֹג בָּהּ הֶרֶג רָב.
1:50 He built a heathen altar in the Temple,	וַיִּבֶן בָּמָה בְּבֵית הַמִּקְדָּשׁ,
1:51 in the place	בַּמָּקוֹם אֲשֶׁר
that the God of Israel said	אָמַר אֱלֹהֵי יִשְׂרָאֵל
1:52 to God's servants, the prophets,	לַעֲבָדָיו הַנְּבִיאִים:
''There shall I cause My Presence to dwell	"שָׁם אֲשַׁכֵּן שְׁכִינָתִי
1:53 forever''; in that	לְעוֹלָם," בַּמָּקוֹם הַהוּא
1:54 very place they slaughtered the swine, and	שָׁחֲטוּ אֶת הַחֲזִיר,
1:55 they brought its blood	וַיָּבִיאוּ אֶת דָּמוֹ
into the holy courtyard.	לְעֶזְרַת הַקֹּדֶשׁ.

P'shat: **1:45. Immediately.** The alacrity with which Antiochus acts points to the high priority he places upon the elimination of Judaism. **1:49–50. great massacre. He built.** The midrash's juxtaposition of the great massacre and the building of the heathen altar alludes to the inherent immorality of idolatrous religion and culture. **1:54. slaughtered.** According to Scripture, a swine carcass causes spiritual defilement, as does the consumption of pig meat (Leviticus 11:7–8). Hence, Nikanor and his henchmen have desecrated the place that the Divine has declared as holy.

D'rash: **1:46. Nikanor, his viceroy.** I and II Maccabees both mention two officers by the name of Nikanor, including one sent to battle forces led by Y'hudah, son of Mattathias. I Maccabees 7:26 describes him as one of the king's "honored princes, who hated and detested Israel." Upon arriving in Jerusalem with a large force, he "treacherously sent to Y'hudah and his brothers this peaceable message, 'Let there be no fighting between you and me. I shall come with a few men to see you face-to-face in peace'" (I Maccabees 7:27–28). In doing so, Nikanor had intended to kidnap Y'hudah. The latter learned of the plot and never went. Having failed at this tactic, Nikanor then engaged the Maccabee forces in battle. Eventually, Y'hudah and his army routed Nikanor and the Syrian-Greeks at Beit-Choron, about fifteen miles northwest of Jerusalem on the thirteenth of Adar, 161 B.C.E. (I Maccabees 7:39–49).[9] The Jews celebrated this day each year as "Nikanor's Day" until the destruction of Jerusalem and the Temple in 70 C.E.[10] II Maccabees 8:9 describes Nikanor as "one of the king's chief Friends," who commanded an army of "no less than twenty-thousand gentiles of all nations, to wipe out the whole race of Judea." The text also informs us that Nikanor had intended to capture some of the Jews and sell them into slavery so that the king could pay the tribute he owed the Romans. **1:48–49. he came to the city of Judah, to Jerusalem.** The Babylonian Talmud (*Taanit* 18b) teaches that every day Nikanor used to raise his hand in threat against Judea's Jerusalem and say, "When will it fall into my hands so that I may trample it to dust?" **1:50. heathen altar.** According to I Maccabees 1:46, Antiochus issued orders to "defile the Sanctuary and the priests." I Maccabees 1:54 speaks of the "desolating sacrilege" that the Syrian-Greeks placed upon the "altar of the burnt offering." Mary Chilton Callaway, in her commentary to I Maccabees,[11] interprets "desolating sacrilege" to refer to a statue of Zeus. The statement of Rava in the Babylonian Talmud, *Avodah Zarah* 42a, corroborates her opinion. According to Jonathan A. Goldstein,[12] Antiochus, in an effort to further erode Jewish sensibilities, required all to refer to God as Zeus Olympius. On the other hand, Elias Bickerman sees this fact as less of an intended affront and more of an attempt on the part of the Greeks to win the Jews over to idolatry, while at the same time providing an image for God that could be understood by the other peoples in the empire. "In this manner the 'God of the Jews' was now accepted into the general pantheon."[13] **1:52. My Presence to dwell.** The Book of Deuteronomy repeatedly refers to "the place where the Eternal your God will choose the divine name to dwell" (16:6, 26:2) and "the place that the Eternal your God will choose" as a central place of worship (12:5, 14:25, 16:15, 18:6). The Rabbis understand the "place" to be none other than the Temple in Jerusalem, as expressed in texts such as the Babylonian Talmud, *Sanhedrin* 11b or *Chulin* 136a. In addition to the desecration of the Jerusalem Temple, I Maccabees 1:54 reports that Antiochus and his forces set up several local altars with the intention of forcing Jews to sacrifice upon them and thus violate the Deuteronomic injunction to sacrifice only at the central Sanctuary. **1:54. slaughtered.** According to I Maccabees 1:59, the first sacrifice upon the heathen altar took place on the twenty-fifth of Kislev. This is, of course, the same date that would eventually mark the beginning of Chanukah, the Festival of Rededication. **1:54–55. swine...brought its blood.** The prophet Isaiah, in condemning those who would attempt to bribe God with insincere offerings, compares these offerings to the bringing of swine's blood into the Sanctuary. Communicating the gravity of sin involved in bringing insincere offerings, he declares, "He who slaughters an ox is as if he slays a man; he who offers a sheep is as if he breaks a dog's neck; he who brings up a meal offering is as if he offers swine's blood; one who brings a frankincense remembrance is as if he brings a gift of extortion—they have chosen their ways, and their souls have desired their abominations" (Isaiah 66:3).

Shabbat, Rosh Chodesh, and Circumcision

The midrash depicts Antiochus issuing a decree against the keeping of Shabbat, Rosh Chodesh, and circumcision in his effort to stamp out Judaism and, hence, destroy the Jewish people. Why in particular does the king lash out against these three observances? Out of the 613 mitzvot (commandments) in the Torah, and thousands of laws and customs delineated in the Talmud and codes, what is it about these three that leads Antiochus, and the author of the midrash, to believe that they hold the key to Jewish continuity?

In answering the above questions, one might initially point to the fact that all three observances enjoy status as biblical mitzvot. In the terminology of the Rabbis, they are *mid'oraita* (מִדְּאוֹרַיְיתָא); that is, Shabbat, Rosh Chodesh, and circumcision are all commanded in the Torah, traditionally regarded as "the word of God" and the sourcebook for Judaism. The Sages, therefore, regard them as elemental, basic to the Jewish enterprise, and carrying much more weight than those observances that owe their origins to popular practice or Rabbinic innovation. Thus, it is only natural that they would be deemed essential to Jewish continuity.

Shabbat

The Torah introduces the seventh day as Shabbat in Genesis 2:1–3, as what might be considered the "crown of Creation." *B'reishit Rabbah* 10:9 likens the divine creation of the world to a king building an adorned bridal chamber. In order to complete the endeavor, the king needed a bride. "So with the world; after the six days of Creation, what was needed to finish it? Shabbat!"

God, following the six days of Creation, rested and blessed and sanctified the seventh day. Rabbi Abraham Joshua Heschel, in his treatise *The Sabbath: Its Meaning for Modern Man,*[14] points out that the first time Scripture refers to holiness, it is in relation to Shabbat. That Shabbat receives over a hundred biblical citations further attests to its great importance in Jewish life.

Two of the most vital of these many allusions arguably occur in the Decalogue, which appears once in Exodus and once in Deuteronomy. We read in Exodus: "Remember the Sabbath day and keep it holy.... For in six days the Eternal made heaven and earth and sea—and all that is in them—and then rested on the seventh day" (20:8, 11). The Rabbis understand this statement as a commandment to imitate God by resting on the seventh day as a remembrance of and witness to the divine role in the work of Creation. Specifically, Jewish tradition regards the statement to "remember" as performing those positive actions that ensure our enjoyment and sanctification of the day, such as making *Kiddush*, the prayer of sanctification uttered over our symbol of joy, wine.

In the Deuteronomy version of the Ten Statements, the Torah commands: "Observe the Sabbath day and keep it holy…Remember that you were a slave in the land of Egypt and the Eternal your God freed you from there with a mighty hand and an outstretched arm" (5:12, 15). The Sages regard this latter version as prohibiting those acts that might be considered "work," utilizing God's role as liberator and redeemer as an underlying paradigm.

Thus, according to Maimonides, Shabbat not only provides physical rest, but represents a theological underpinning to Judaism. Its observance bears witness to Creation, "which at once and clearly leads to the theory of the existence of God," and to the role of divine "kindness" in effecting the Exodus from Egypt (*Guide for the Perplexed* 2:31).

On another level, as Rabbi Ephraim Buchwald points out, Shabbat represents a sense of wholeness in that it refreshes on both biological and social levels. Shabbat is connected to Creation in that human beings, like other life forms with whom we share our planet, require work and physical rest (both a systolic and a diastolic phase, a contraction and a letting go, work and relaxation) in order to most effectively carry on. The Exodus, the redemption from the people-made institution of slavery, when applied to Shabbat reminds us that the seventh day is one consecrated to human relationship. It is a day to clear one's schedule in order to achieve quality time with those we love, by creating an island of quantity time.[15]

In addition, the Torah refers to the seventh day as a "Sabbath of the Eternal your God" (Exodus 20:10). Shabbat may be seen as a time to cultivate our spiritual relationship with the Divine. It is the day to nurture the religious connection that undergirds the continuity of the Jewish people and fuels our mission to bring healing to the world. Unencumbered by the demands of commerce, Shabbat becomes the day of prayer and Torah study par excellence.

Rosh Chodesh

Exodus 12:2 states: "This month shall mark for you the beginning of the months." Rashi cites an ancient midrash, the *M'chilta*, when he comments that the term "this" implies that God is actually showing Moses the new moon to indicate that it must be sanctified for the new month to ensue. This proves vital, as without the declaration of the New Moon, there is no month (the Hebrew word for "month," חֹדֶשׁ, *chodesh*, also means "moon") and, hence, no Hebrew calendar. The Hebrew calendar serves as the basis of Jewish culture and religion. Without the calendar, the holy Festivals, commanded to the Jewish people through the Torah, cannot be fulfilled, as we read in Leviticus 23:4: "These are the set times of the Eternal [מוֹעֲדֵי יְהֹוָה, *mo-adei Adonai*], the sacred occasions, which you shall celebrate each at its appointed time."

The commandment to sanctify the New Moon represents Jewish peoplehood, as it is the first mitzvah given to the nation as a whole. Unlike Shabbat, which is counted by each individual, according to the Mishnah, Rosh Chodesh can only be proclaimed by the Sanhedrin, the high court that regulated all religious affairs in ancient days (see *Mishnah Rosh HaShanah* 2:7). The one who controls the calendar, in other words, controls society. By outlawing Rosh Chodesh, Antiochus attempts not only to abrogate the Hebrew calendar and eliminate the Festivals of the Jewish year, but to completely usurp the authority of the high court and outstrip the religious leadership of the Jewish people.

Circumcision

Like Shabbat and Rosh Chodesh, the practice of the covenant of circumcision (בְּרִית מִילָה, *b'rit milah*) is most ancient. According to author Anita Diamant, it is the "oldest continuing Jewish rite, a ritual that unites Jews throughout ages and across cultures and signifies the connection between individual human life and the Holy."[16] Diamant also points out that circumcision has become so associated with the covenant in the eyes of the people that Jews colloquially refer to its occurrence as a "bris," literally, covenant.

The Torah initially reveals the commandment to circumcise in its depiction of God's message to Abraham: "Let every male among you be circumcised.... It shall become a sign of the covenant between us" (Genesis 17:10–11). Scripture further prescribes that the rite be accomplished on the eighth day of a male baby's life (Genesis 17:12; Leviticus 12:3).

Circumcision is at once a sign of the covenant, Jewish identity, and membership in the Jewish nation. Its significance as such is attested to by the fact that in order to participate in the ritual of the paschal sacrifice, the birthday of the Jewish people, as it were, a man must be circumcised (Exodus 12:48). Indeed, one of the necessary steps that a prospective convert must traditionally undertake to become a full-fledged member of the Jewish people is circumcision.

In addition, there is a mystical aspect associated with circumcision. In introducing the commandment of circumcision to Abraham, the Torah depicts God telling the patriarch to "walk before Me and be perfect" (Genesis 17:1). Hence, an ancient midrash (*B'reishit Rabbah* 46:4) associates the removal of the foreskin with perfection. Another midrash focuses upon the miracle of life that may be performed by the organ of circumcision (*B'reishit Rabbah* 46:2). This act of continuity is, of course, performed in partnership, not only with woman, but with God.

The Mishnah (*N'darim* 3:11) records the opinion of Rabbi Y'hudah HaNasi that circumcision carries so much weight, it is the equivalent of all the other commandments combined! About the nature of the mitzvot, Rabbi Lawrence Kushner writes, "When we perform a mitzvah, we make it ours. We understand it; we 'hear' it. It becomes a part of us. Performing a mitzvah changes us, brings us closer to God. It also has the mysterious power to repair what is broken."[17] Therefore circumcision, as the equivalent of all of the mitzvot combined, carries with it the ability to transform us as human beings, to spiritually lift us to a closer relationship with the Divine, and to somehow, quite mysteriously, make this world a better place by guaranteeing the continuity of the Jewish people as God's covenantal partners.

Conclusions

In considering and reconsidering the question of why these three particular practices, Shabbat, Rosh Chodesh, and circumcision, prove to be so vital to Jewish continuity, one may imagine them coming together like the pieces of a pie, to represent all the cycles of life.

Shabbat, arriving every seventh day, represents the weekly cycle. Rosh Chodesh, in its connection to the movements of the moon and the establishment of the Hebrew calendar, relates to the monthly, yearly, and holiday cycles. Circumcision is a life-cycle event. Together, these three mitzvot constitute the Jewish concept of sacred time and our place within it.

These three mitzvot again represent a totality when one considers that together their observance involves the entire population. Circumcision is, of course, only associated with males in Judaism. A sign of the covenant sealed in the flesh of the male organ, the tradition regards the father as being responsible for its performance. Thus, its practice may be regarded as an avenue to a kind of male bonding that flows from one generation to the next.

Women have traditionally enjoyed a special relationship with Rosh Chodesh. The *Shulchan Aruch*, for instance, cites the time-honored custom of women refraining from work on Rosh Chodesh. In modern times, many women's prayer and Torah study groups have grown up around the observance of Rosh Chodesh. Some scholars have noted a parallel between the lunar cycle and that of women's fertility. Thus, each new moon may be regarded as a symbol of the renewal of the opportunity to carry the banner of Judaism into the next generation.

Many regard Shabbat as "family time." Jewish tradition considers Shabbat to represent the coming together of male and female. A famous midrash refers to the seventh day as a bride and Israel as its groom (see Gleanings, "Israel's Mate"). The kabbalists regard Shabbat as a "taste of the world-to-come," in that the unification of God's name is achieved on this day. That is, the male and the female aspects of the godhead unite in oneness on the sacred Sabbath. Sexual intercourse, then, becomes one of the metaphors for the divine unity manifest on Shabbat.

In addition, it should be noted that all three mitzvot, circumcision, Rosh Chodesh, and Shabbat, present occasions for communal gathering. Hence, their observances in actuality involve not only individual males and females of all ages, as mentioned above, but the Jewish community as a whole.

It is also important to note that all three observances combine to form some of the most vital and basic theological underpinnings of Judaism. To observe Shabbat is to bear witness to God as Creator and Redeemer. As the *Kiddush*, the prayer of Sabbath sanctification, declares, "It is a memorial to the acts of Creation...a memory to the Exodus of Egypt." The experiences of Egypt, slavery and redemption, function as the subtext of the commandments that regulate our conduct toward our fellow human beings and advise our relationship with the Divine.

Circumcision points to God's role as Revealer. It reminds us that God stipulates the terms of the covenant in prophetic encounter with the seers of our people, as recorded in our Holy Scripture.

Rosh Chodesh alludes to the role of the Jewish people as God's eternal servants. The moon cyclically shines, seems to fade, only to shine again; so too the many phases of the Jewish people. We have experienced eras of "light and joy, gladness and honor" (Esther 8:16), and we have known times of darkness. There have been epochs of power and periods of persecution. Yet, every time it seemed the Jewish people would fade from the scene, like the new moon that suddenly reappears and then grows larger and brighter, we have reemerged, reenergized, and rededicated ourselves to our sacred mission of healing the world. Those powerful empires that oppressed us (Egypt, Assyria, Babylonia, Greece, Rome) may have shined brightly for a moment in history. But the sands of time extinguished their lights long ago. Their civilizations have turned to dust. The Jewish people, on the other hand, marches into the future carrying high the torch of God's kindness, ever kindling and rededicating the menorah of divine justice and morality. "David, king of Israel, lives and endures!"[18]

17

Hence, the Rabbis chose these three mitzvot, Shabbat, Rosh Chodesh, and circumcision, to be outlawed by Antiochus in *M'gillat Antiochus*, for removing them would undermine Judaism. Together, their practice holds the power to promote and refine our relationships with both God and our fellow human beings. This holds especially true for those who actively participate in the Jewish community, for Shabbat, Rosh Chodesh, and circumcision all provide settings for the communal gathering and sharing of acts of loving-kindness that ultimately prove to be the characteristic tenets and responsibilities of Judaism.

Finally, in considering the important roles that Shabbat, Rosh Chodesh, and circumcision play in Jewish continuity, one must mention their relationship to time. Shabbat represents the weekly cycle, the unending Jewish commitment to create holiness in time by dedicating a day to God's purpose, a day that includes prayer and Torah learning. Rosh Chodesh represents the calendar of the Jewish year. The Festivals that grace this annual cycle tie its adherents to the Land, as each celebrates another agricultural event taking place in the Land of Israel. The Festivals also celebrate the major events in Jewish history, thus facilitating continuity by continually causing the Jewish people to acknowledge their common heritage. Circumcision as accomplished on the eighth day of a child's life represents the Jewish hope for the future, as each child born into the world and committed to the covenant bears the potential to grow to contribute to the mission of Israel, to make this world a better and more peaceful place.

GLEANINGS

1:1–2 "It happened in the days of Antiochus, king of Greece..."

Hellenism versus Judaism

No gymnasium could be without the images of such patron gods of athletics as Heracles and without honorific statues of the kings. Every public act was invariably accompanied by sacrifice and invariably involved prayer. To accept Western culture fully, therefore, there appeared no other alternatives than either to renounce the ancestral religion, to which any participation in the cult of the gods was an abomination, or to transform the ancient law.

Elias Bickerman, *From Ezra to the Last of the Maccabees*, p. 108

1:32–34 "Then we will have control over the sea and dry land, so that the entire world will be given into our hand."

The Deadliest Form

In the winter of 1945...I began to suspect that the deadliest form of antisemitism, the kind that results in massacre and attempted genocide, has little to do with real conflicts of interest between living people, or even with racial prejudice as such. What I kept coming across was, rather, a conviction that Jews– all Jews everywhere in the world—form a conspiratorial body set on ruining and then dominating the rest of mankind.

Norman Cohn, *Warrant for Genocide*, p. xii

1:39–41 "We will nullify the covenant God made with them: Sabbath, New Moon, and circumcision."

Architecture of Time

Jewish ritual may be characterized as the art of significant forms in time, as *architecture*

of time. Most of its observances—the Sabbath, the New Moon, the festivals, the Sabbatical and the Jubilee year—depend on a certain hour of the day or season of the year.... The main themes of faith lie in the realm of time. We remember the day of the exodus from Egypt, the day when Israel stood at Sinai; and our Messianic hope is the expectation of a day, of the end of days.

Abraham Joshua Heschel, *The Sabbath: Its Meaning for Modern Man*, p. 8

1:40–41 "Sabbath, New Moon, and circumcision"

Israel's Mate

Rabbi Shimon ben Yochai taught: Shabbat said before the Holy One, blessed be God, "Master of the universe, everyone has a mate, but I have no mate." The Holy One, blessed be God, answered, "The Community of Israel shall be your mate." Thus, when Israel stood before Mount Sinai, the Holy One, blessed be God, said to them, "Remember the thing I said to Shabbat, that the Community of Israel will be your mate." Hence, it says (Exodus 20:8), "Remember the Sabbath day and keep it holy."

B'reishit Rabbah 11:8

Sabbath Prayer

God, help us now to make this new Shabbat.
After noise, we seek quiet;
After crowds of indifferent strangers,
We seek to touch those we love;
After concentration on work and responsibility,
We seek freedom to meditate, to listen to our inward selves.
We open our eyes to the hidden beauties
and the infinite possibilities in the world You are creating;

We break open the gates of the reservoirs
of goodness and kindness in ourselves and in
    others;
We reach toward one holy perfect moment
    of Shabbat.

Ruth Brin, in *Gates of Shabbat:*
A Guide for Observing Shabbat, p. 79

Equivalent to All the Commandments

Rabbi Levi said: If Israel kept Shabbat properly even for one day, the son of David would come. Why? Because it is the equivalent of all the commandments; as it says, "For God is our God, and we are the people of God's pasture, and the flock of God's hand. Today, if you would but hearken to God's voice" (Psalm 95:7).

Sh'mot Rabbah 25:12

Renewed Like the Moon

The women heard about the construction of the Golden Calf and refused to submit their jewelry to their husbands. Instead, they said to them, "You want to construct an idol and mask which is an abomination and has no power of redemption? We won't listen to you." And the Holy One, blessed be God, rewarded them in this world in that they would observe the new moons more than men, and in the next world in that they are destined to be renewed like the new moons.

Pirkei D'Rabbi Eliezer 45

Symbol of Renewal

Rosh Hodesh is a symbol of renewal. At the end of its monthly cycle, the moon becomes visually obliterated, only to re-appear as a tiny, luminous sliver of light as it commences a fresh, new cycle. Likewise, we have the opportunity to take stock of our lives and revise our behavior, our commitments, our goals. We, too, have the power to start over.

Leora Tanenbaum, Claudia R. Chernov,
and Hadassah Tropper, *Moonbeams:*
A Hadassah Rosh Hodesh Guide, p. 1

Limits to Everything

Circumcision teaches that there are limits to everything. Men especially need to hear this. We do not single-handedly control everything. The world is not completely ours. A piece of us belongs to God. After all, when God revealed the Divine Self to Abram, God's Name is revealed as El Shaddai. El Shaddai can be translated as the God Who said, "*Dai!* Enough! There are limits to what you can do in your life!"

Jeffrey K. Salkin, *Searching for My Brothers*,
p. 177

Renewal in Each Generation

The *brit milah*, the "covenant of the circumcision," becomes the totem of this family's alliance with God, marked indelibly in the flesh of each of its men.... Though this covenant is everlasting, it must be renewed in each generation by the father circumcising his sons in memory of the historical link to his forefathers, and to God.

Naomi H. Rosenblatt and Joshua Horwitz,
Wrestling with Angels, pp. 152–53

Why Should I Circumcise My Son?

The significance and ritual power of *brit milah* is not the stuff of reason, or even of language. This is a radical act of faith, as well as a tangible, physical, visceral connection to our most ancient past. The simplest, most compelling answer to the question of why we do this to our sons is this: if we stop doing *brit milah* we stop being Jews as we have been since Abraham.

Anita Diamant, *The New Jewish Baby Book*, p. 95

Chapter 2

Zeal versus Passivity: Yochanan Takes Action

Jewish tradition reveals that life is never simple. People conflict, and often so do values. While Judaism teaches the sanctity of human life, and the Torah explicitly commands, "You shall not murder" (Exodus 20:13), the evils of our yet unredeemed world beg a proper response. The Talmud rules that one may stop a murderer from committing a crime, even at the cost of the murderer's life (*Sanhedrin* 72a). Killing a potential murderer when there is no other option available is not considered murder (the unjustified taking of innocent life), but self-defense.

At certain critical moments in history, egregious evils and the challenges to survival that they pose engender and arguably justify extraordinary measures of self-defense to stop them. For example, Adolph Hitler's murderous World War II rampage moved German minister and theologian Dietrich Bonhoeffer to become involved in a plot that involved placing an explosive-packed suitcase at the Führer's feet during a staff meeting. Bonhoeffer's goal was to save millions of innocent human lives.

In this chapter Yochanan, Mattathias's son, judges the massacre of the Jewish people and desecration of the holy Temple perpetrated by Nikanor to constitute a threat, not only to millions of innocent lives in his own day, but to the very survival of Judaism and the Jewish people. Weighing the consequences, Yochanan decides that he cannot stand idly by. Rather, he must take radical action for the sake of the Jewish people and survival of their faith.

Yochanan's actions speak to us of the extraordinary circumstances posed by genocidal tyrants who would slaughter the innocent. But the lessons of Yochanan's deeds also bear wider application, for they teach the value of an active approach in meeting the challenges represented by the great social action issues of our own day, as well as those personal obstacles that hinder us from becoming the people we may yet be. Just as Yochanan expresses anger and rage at the problems Nikanor poses, positive change in our world and in our lives must begin with a certain dissatisfaction with the status quo. Yochanan's righteous outrage propels him to act, and so must we utilize our respect for what is right and our love of justice to motivate ourselves to take

21

action if we are to heal the world and improve ourselves. These challenges don't require the kind of violent behavior exhibited by Yochanan in this chapter. Rather, one must analyze each individual situation to arrive at an appropriate plan of action. The midrash merely teaches that passivity can be counterproductive to our goals of self-improvement, Jewish continuity, and *tikkun olam* (healing the world). Hence, this chapter introduces one of the great themes of Chanukah, that of taking action.

2:1	And because of this,	וּבִהְיוֹת זֶה,
	when Yochanan the son	כַּאֲשֶׁר שָׁמַע יוֹחָנָן
2:2	of Mattathias heard of this deed that was	בֶּן מַתִּתְיָה כִּי זֶה הַמַּעֲשֶׂה
2:3	committed, he became filled with	נַעֲשָׂה, נִמְלָא
	anger and rage,	קֶצֶף וְחֵמָה,
2:4	and the color of his face changed,	וְזִיו פָּנָיו נִשְׁתַּנָּה,
2:5	and he contemplated what he would be able	וַיִּוָּעֵץ בְּלִבּוֹ מַה שֶּׁיָּכוֹל
2:6	to do about it.	לַעֲשׂוֹת עַל זֶה.
	And then Yochanan, the son of	וְאָז יוֹחָנָן בֶּן
2:7	Mattathias, made a sword for himself,	מַתִּתְיָה עָשָׂה לוֹ חֶרֶב
2:8	two spans in length	שְׁתֵּי זְרָתוֹת אָרְכָּהּ
2:9	and one span in width,	וְזֶרֶת אַחַת רָחְבָּהּ,
2:10	and concealed it beneath his clothes.	וְהִיא תַּחַת בְּגָדָיו עֲטוּפָה.

P'shat: **2:1. And because of this.** That is, the twin tragedy of the massacre and the desecration of the holy Temple. Unlike Antiochus, whose motivation and actions stem from his own ego, the needs of his people and the requirements of the covenant galvanize Yochanan to action. **2:4. color of his face.** This indicates the deep-seated nature of Yochanan's passion for justice; extreme emotion can cause one's face to redden. **2:5. contemplated.** Although fueled by righteous indignation, Yochanan's actions are not the result of a spur of the moment expression of uncontrollable rage. Rather, Yochanan's response to the Temple's desecration and the slaughter of the innocent is the result of careful preparation. **2:7. made a sword for himself.** Making the sword himself would be one way to keep the entire matter a secret. **2:8–9. two spans in length and one span in width.** A span equals three handbreadths, or approximately 10.6 inches (27 centimeters).[1] Thus, Yochanan's concealed sword measures about 21.2 inches in length and 10.6 inches wide!

D'rash: **2:1. And because of this.** While the massacre wrought by Antiochus obviously threatens Jewish existence on the physical level, the desecration of the Temple represents their spiritual demise. **2:1–2. Yochanan, the son of Mattathias.** *M'gillat Antiochus* reflects the tradition that Yochanan was one of five brothers: Yochanan, Y'hudah, Yonatan, Elazar, and Shimon. Together with their father they were known as the Hasmoneans. According to Josephus (*Antiquities* 12.6.1), the family took its name from Mattathias's great-grandfather, Hasmoneus. Yochanan, his father, and his brothers are also frequently referred to as the Maccabees (see *d'rash* commentary on 2:76). **2:1–2. when Yochanan the son of Mattathias heard.** Yochanan's hearing echoes Pinchas's "seeing" in the case of his act of zealotry, killing a royal couple as they copulated publicly, as depicted in Numbers 25:7–8: "When Pinchas, son of Eleazar son of Aaron the priest, *saw* this, he left the assembly and, taking a spear in his hand, he followed the Israelite into the chamber and stabbed both of them." The Rabbis of the Talmud (*Sanhedrin* 82a) enquire as to what exactly Pinchas saw. They provide three different answers: First, they posit that Moses proved ineffectual at this point in his career. Therefore, someone had to step up and do something to put an end to the idolatrous orgy that threatened the existence of Judaism at this early point in its history. Pinchas rightly took charge. Second, the Sages opine that Pinchas saw Zimri, a prince from the tribe of Shimon, publicly copulating with a Midianite princess named Cozbi. This outrage prompted Pinchas to make a plan of action. The third answer teaches that Pinchas saw the Angel of Death bringing a plague upon the people as a result of their immoral behavior with Moabite and Midianite women, who enticed the Children of Israel to idolatrous practice by seducing them sexually. In this view, the fact that Zimri and Cozbi were royalty served as a symbol of encouragement for the people to sin. By sacrificing the lives of these two high-profile profligates, Pinchas saved the rest of the people. Similarly, one may deduce that Yochanan hopes that by killing Nikanor, he will save the rest of the people. **2:7. made a sword for himself.** This echoes Judges 3:16–21, which depicts Ehud crafting a double-edged sword and concealing it beneath his raiment as he meets with the Moabite king, Eglon. The fact that both Ehud and Yochanan make their own swords points to their zeal to perform their religious duties. This may be compared to Abraham saddling his own donkey in response to God's command that he take Isaac to the land of Moriah when a servant could have done this (Genesis 22:3). See also Psalm 149:6–7, which depicts the triumph of the faithful, "Let the praises of God be in their mouths and a double-edged sword in their hands, for avenging the nations, to work chastisements upon the peoples." While *B'midbar Rabbah* 11:3 interprets the psalm's double-edged sword figuratively to represent the Torah, the study and observance of which tame the nations' darker passions and put an end to their immorality,[2] Dr. Marc Brettler comments, "The ideal presented here is not quietistic piety, but faith combined with military action. God will avenge the nations, but only by coming to the aid of the pious as together they vanquish their common enemy."[3] The Talmud, in its discussion of the zealotry of Pinchas (*Sanhedrin* 82a–b), explains that like Yochanan and Ehud, Pinchas also acted with cunning. That is, he removed the metal tip of his spear and placed it beneath his garment. Approaching the tribe of Shimon, where Zimri and Cozbi carried on, Pinchas utilized the shaft of his spear as a walking stick. He then led the Shimonites to believe that he had come to participate in the idolatrous orgy, in order to draw close to the offending couple.

2:11	He came to Jerusalem, and stood in	וַיָּבוֹא לִירוּשָׁלַיִם, וַיַּעֲמֹד
2:12	the gate of the king, and called to the	בְּשַׁעַר הַמֶּלֶךְ, וַיִּקְרָא
2:13	gatekeepers and said to them, "I am	לַשּׁוֹעֲרִים וַיֹּאמֶר לָהֶם: "אֲנִי
2:14	Yochanan, the son of Mattathias,	יוֹחָנָן בֶּן מַתִּתְיָה,
2:15	the High Priest of the Jews;	הַכֹּהֵן הַגָּדוֹל שֶׁל הַיְּהוּדִים.
	I have come	בָּאתִי
2:16	to appear before Nikanor."	לָבוֹא לִפְנֵי נִיקָנוֹר."
2:17	Then, the gatekeepers and the guards came	וְאָז בָּאוּ הַשּׁוֹעֲרִים וְהַשּׁוֹמְרִים
2:18	and said to Nikanor,	וַיֹּאמְרוּ לְנִיקָנוֹר:
2:19	"The High Priest of the Jews is	"הַכֹּהֵן הַגָּדוֹל מֵהַיְּהוּדִים
2:20	standing at the entrance."	עוֹמֵד בַּפֶּתַח."
2:21	Nikanor answered and said to them,	וַיַּעַן נִיקָנוֹר וַיֹּאמֶר לָהֶם:
2:22	"Let him enter."	"בּוֹא יָבוֹא."

***P'shat*: 2:11. He came to Jerusalem.** Mattathias and his five sons, Yochanan, Y'hudah, Shimon, Yonatan, and Elazar, had fled Jerusalem to reside in Modi'in, a small town located thirty thousand cubits (approximately 8.5–11.3 miles) outside of the capital city (Babylonian Talmud, *P'sachim* 96b). **2:12. gate of the king.** Apparently one of the entrances to the Temple complex. Nikanor, the governor, in his arrogance, had further desecrated the holy place by commandeering it as his residence and headquarters. **2:19. The High Priest of the Jews.** The phrase literally means the High Priest from the Jews; implying that the Syrian-Greeks of the palace in their hubris might have assumed Yochanan to have been sent on official business by the Jews perhaps to negotiate surrender.

***D'rash*: 2:15. the High Priest of the Jews.** Many historians regard Yochanan's claim to be the High Priest with skepticism. According to Josephus, in the century before these events, the line of the High Priesthood stretched from Shimon the Righteous to his son Chunya II, to Shimon II, to Chunya III. Antiochus then deposed Chunya III, politicized the position, and made the High Priest a tax farmer, that is, one authorized by the royal government to collect taxes in its name. In Chunya III's stead, Antiochus appointed the Hellenizer Jason. Menelaus, an even more extreme Hellenizer, then overthrew Jason to become the royally sanctioned High Priest. To further complicate matters, some sources, including the standard version of the *Al HaNisim* prayer, refer to Mattathias, son of Yochanan, as the High Priest. Our verse above may be parsed to indicate that Yochanan was the son of the High Priest, Mattathias.[4] Josephus (*Antiquities* 12.6) reports the name of Mattathias's grandfather to have been Shimon. Could he have been Shimon II, and Chunya III short for Yochanan?[5] Maimonides, in the sixth chapter of his preface to *Seder Z'raim* (of the Mishnah)[6] states that the Yochanan the High Priest who is mentioned in *Mishnah Maaseir Sheini* 5:15 was the son of Mattathias the Hasmonean. The use of the title here in *M'gillat Antiochus* by Yochanan, Mattathias's son, then, may be understood in the sense of righteous protest. That is, Yochanan identifies himself as High Priest as a protest against the corruption of the office brought about by the king's involvement in what should be an internal Jewish religious matter. As opposed to Antiochus, whose concern for his own power and ego drives his behavior, Yochanan operates from a purely religious motive.

2:23	Then Yochanan was brought before	אָז הוּבָא יוֹחָנָן לִפְנֵי
2:24	Nikanor. Nikanor spoke up	נִיקָנוֹר. וַיַּעַן נִיקָנוֹר
	and said to Yochanan,	וַיֹּאמֶר לְיוֹחָנָן:
2:25	"You are one of the rebels who	"אַתָּה הוּא אֶחָד מִן הַמּוֹרְדִים
2:26	rebelled against the king and who do not	אֲשֶׁר מָרְדוּ בַּמֶּלֶךְ וְאֵינָם
2:27	care about the welfare of his kingdom."	רוֹצִים בִּשְׁלוֹם מַלְכוּתוֹ."
2:28	Yochanan spoke up before Nikanor and	וַיַּעַן יוֹחָנָן לִפְנֵי נִיקָנוֹר
2:29	said, "My lord, now I have come	וַיֹּאמֶר: "אֲדוֹנִי, עַתָּה בָאתִי
2:30	before you; that which you desire	לְפָנֶיךָ, אֲשֶׁר תִּרְצֶה
2:31	I will do."	אֶעֱשֶׂה."
2:32	Nikanor spoke up and said to Yochanan,	וַיַּעַן נִיקָנוֹר וַיֹּאמֶר לְיוֹחָנָן:
2:33	"If you will do according to my will, take	"אִם כִּרְצוֹנִי אַתָּה עוֹשֶׂה, קַח
2:34	a swine and slay it upon the heathen altar;	חֲזִיר וּשְׁחָטֵהוּ עַל הַבָּמָה,
2:35	and you will wear royal clothing,	וְתִלְבַּשׁ בִּגְדֵי מַלְכוּת,
2:36	and you will ride upon the king's horse,	וְתִרְכַּב עַל סוּס הַמֶּלֶךְ,
2:37	and you will be one of the Friends	וּכְאֶחָד מֵאוֹהֲבֵי
	of the King."	הַמֶּלֶךְ תִּהְיֶה."

P'shat: 2:24, 28. spoke up...spoke up. Yochanan shows his courage by speaking up, just as the governor had. **2:29–30. My lord, now I have come before you.** Yochanan plays upon Nikanor's ego, implying that being in the great man's presence has swayed his allegiance. **2:33–34. take a swine and slay it upon the heathen altar.** This would constitute an obvious act of apostasy.

D'rash: 2:33–34. take a swine and slay it upon the heathen altar. According to the account of I Maccabees 2:27, the Hasmonean revolt began with an incident surrounding the slaughter of a swine on one of the local altars set up by the Syrian-Greeks. Upon witnessing a Jew sacrifice a swine under the authority of a Syrian-Greek officer, Mattathias killed the man and the officer and rallied the people: "All who are zealous for the sake of the Torah, who uphold the covenant, march out after me!" Thus, by ordering him to sacrifice the swine, Nikanor demands that Yochanan not only violate the tenets of Judaism, but also repudiate his father and the very foundations of the uprising. **2:35–36. You will wear royal clothing, and you will ride upon the king's horse.** This echoes Esther 6:11, which depicts King Ahasuerus rewarding Mordechai for having saved his life by having him dressed in royal clothing and paraded upon the king's horse. **2:37. one of the Friends of the King.** According to Mary Chilton Calloway,[7] the "Friends of the King" was an official order of preferred citizens. Yochanan's membership would indicate his arrival in Hellenized society.

2:38	And when Yochanan heard, he	וְכַאֲשֶׁר שָׁמַע יוֹחָנָן,
2:39	replied, "My lord, I am afraid of the	הֵשִׁיבוֹ דָבָר: "אֲדוֹנִי אֲנִי יָרֵא
2:40	Children of Israel, lest they hear	מִבְּנֵי יִשְׂרָאֵל, פֶּן יִשְׁמְעוּ
2:41	that I have done such and stone me;	כִּי עָשִׂיתִי כֵן וְיִסְקְלוּנִי בָּאֲבָנִים;
2:42	now let every man go out from before	עַתָּה יֵצֵא כָל אִישׁ מִלְפָנֶיךָ,
2:43	you, lest they inform the Children of	פֶּן יוֹדִיעוּ לִבְנֵי
2:44	Israel."	יִשְׂרָאֵל."
2:45	Then Nikanor sent every man from	אָז הוֹצִיא נִיקָנוֹר
2:46	his presence. At that moment	מִלְפָנָיו כָּל אִישׁ. בָּעֵת הַהִיא
2:47	Yochanan raised his eyes to the	נָשָׂא יוֹחָנָן בֶּן מַתִּתְיָה עֵינָיו
2:48	heavens and prayed	לַשָּׁמַיִם, וְתִקֵּן תְּפִלָּתוֹ
2:49	before the Ruler of the worlds and said,	לִפְנֵי רִבּוֹן הָעוֹלָמִים וַיֹּאמַר:
2:50	"My God and God of my ancestors,	"אֱלֹהַי וֵאלֹהֵי אֲבוֹתַי,
2:51	Abraham, Isaac, and Jacob,	אַבְרָהָם יִצְחָק וְיַעֲקֹב

2:52 please do not give me over	אַל נָא תִּתְּנֵנִי בְּיַד
to this uncircumcised heathen.	הֶעָרֵל הַזֶּה,
2:53 For if he kills	כִּי אִם יַהַרְגֵנִי
2:54 me, he will go and worship in the	יֵלֵךְ וְיִשְׁתַּבַּח
2:55 temple of Dagon his god and say,	בְּבֵית דָּגוֹן אֱלֹהָיו וְיֹאמַר:
2:56 'My god gave him over to my hand.'"	'אֱלֹהַי נְתָנוּ בְיָדִי.'"

P'shat: **2:38. And when Yochanan heard.** The Hebrew term שָׁמַע (*shama*) not only means "he heard," but also implies that "he understood" the impact of Nikanor's request. Yochanan also understands at this point exactly what he would have to do. **2:45–46. Nikanor sent every man from his presence.** Nikanor seems to believe that his palace security and his stature as the king's general and viceroy would protect him from any harm, an indication of his hubris in his denial of divine power.[8] **2:48. prayed.** This, again, indicates the purity of Yochanan's motives. Not animated by some prospect of personal vengeance, Yochanan acts solely as God's instrument of justice. **2:53–55. For if he kills me, he will go and worship in the temple of Dagon his god.** Yochanan does not pray for God's help for the sake of his own merit. Rather, he implores God to help him lest his demise spell a victory for idolatry and a diminution of God's presence and influence in this world. This statement is an indication of Yochanan's humility.

D'rash: **2:45–46. Nikanor sent every man from his presence.** This again echoes the actions of Ehud in the days of the Judges. When Ehud informs Eglon, the Moabite king, that he has a secret matter to share with him, the latter orders all to leave his presence. Ehud declares, "I have a message from God to you." He then pulls out the concealed sword he made and thrusts it deep into the king's belly (Judges 3:19–21). **2:51. Abraham, Isaac, and Jacob.** Yochanan's prayer proves reminiscent of the *Avot*, the first blessing of the *Amidah*: "the God of Abraham, the God of Jacob, and the God of Isaac." The *Amidah*, the central Rabbinic prayer of the Jewish worship service, is that rubric into which the *Al HaNisim* of Chanukah is inserted. This first blessing alludes to our relationship with God, a relationship that began many years ago with the Patriarchs and continues into the future. Yochanan's alluding to the Patriarchs in prayer also echoes Jacob's prayer on the evening before he must face his brother Esau, who vowed to kill him when they last met twenty years before (Genesis 32:10–12). Both Yochanan and Jacob recognize God's role in their deliverance, a sign of their humility. The Talmud (*M'gillah* 11a) associates humility with righteousness.

2:52. this uncircumcised heathen. David uses this term to refer to Goliath, the champion of the Philistines, Israel's enemy (I Samuel 17:36). David's slaying of the Philistine giant is followed by an Israelite rout of the Philistine army (I Samuel 17:51–53). Here the term not only places Nikanor into a similar category as that of Goliath, the anti-Jewish heathen and a member of a people that scholars assert originated in the Aegean basin and invaded from across the sea,[9] but the mention of circumcision echoes Antiochus's decree against it. Hence, the use of the term serves as a criticism of those Hellenizing Jews who have heeded Antiochus's decree to become anti-Jewish "heathens" themselves.[10] **2:55. Dagon his god.** Dagon was a god of the Philistines. Its mention here may be part of an effort to place the story of Chanukah within a biblical context, despite the fact that the historical events of Chanukah took place after the close of the biblical era. **2:56. My god gave him over to my hand.** The argument that Yochanan employs is similar to that of Moses, who responds to God's desire to destroy the Jewish people after the "sin of the spies": "The nations . . . will say, 'It must be because the Eternal was powerless to bring that people into the land promised them on oath that [that God] slaughtered them in the wilderness'" (Numbers 14:15–16). Thus, the battle against Nikanor may be understood to have theological implications and, as was the case with Moses, constitutes a test of Yochanan's leadership. Both Moses and Yochanan, having passed the divine test, emerge as stronger, more capable leaders.

2:57 At that moment he advanced three	בְּאוֹתָהּ שָׁעָה פָּסַע עָלָיו שָׁלֹשׁ
2:58 steps toward him, thrust the sword	פְּסִיעוֹת, וַיִּתְקַע הַחֶרֶב
2:59 into his heart, and flung him mortally	בְּלִבּוֹ, וַיַּשְׁלֵךְ אוֹתוֹ חָלָל
2:60 wounded into the holy court.	בְּעֶזְרַת הַקֹּדֶשׁ.
2:61 Yochanan spoke up and said before	עָנָה יוֹחָנָן וְאָמַר לִפְנֵי
2:62 the God of the heavens, "My God, do	אֱלֹהֵי הַשָּׁמַיִם: "אֱלֹהַי אַל
2:63 not count it against me as a sin that I	תָּשֶׁם עָלַי חֵטְא כִּי
2:64 killed this uncircumcised heathen	הָרַגְתִּי אֶת הֶעָרֵל הַזֶּה
2:65 in the Temple; now may You give over	בְּבֵית הַמִּקְדָּשׁ, כֵּן תִּתֵּן עַתָּה אֶת
2:66 all the peoples that came with him to	כָּל הָעַמִּים אֲשֶׁר בָּאוּ עִמּוֹ
2:67 persecute Judah and Jerusalem."	לְהָצֵר לִיהוּדָה וְלִירוּשָׁלָיִם."

***P'shat*: 2:62–63. My God, do not count it against me as a sin.** Under normal circumstances, one is not permitted to kill another human being within the precincts of the Temple, even to carry out a lawful capital sentence of the court. In addition to ethical concerns, the presence of a corpse will render ritual impurity.[10] In fact, the builders of the Temple would not even wield iron tools in its construction, as weapons are also made of iron, thus emphasizing the role of the holy Temple as a symbol of peace.

D'rash: 2:58–59 thrust the sword into his heart. According to Rava (as cited in Babylonian Talmud, *B'rachot* 63a), such a course of action is supported by Psalm 119:126, "It is time to act for the Eternal." That is, there are situations when, for the greater good, in order to perform a divine deed, one that furthers God's purpose, a law of the Torah may be transgressed. **2:59–60. flung him mortally wounded.** I Maccabees 7:43 reports that Y'hudah, son of Mattathias, and his army killed Nikanor in battle at Beit-Choron. In fact, Nikanor was the first to fall in that battle. According to Josephus, Nikanor proved to be the final casualty of that battle (*Antiquities* 10.4). The anniversary of his falling, the thirteenth of Adar (I Maccabees 7:49; II Maccabees 15:36), came to be celebrated each year as a minor holiday, during which fasting and eulogies were forbidden (*M'gillat Taanit*, mishnah 30). **2:66. Peoples.** The term employed here, עַמִּים (*amim*), "peoples," is related to גּוֹיִם (*goyim*), connoting the nations of the world (all those besides Israel). Thus, Yochanan's battles pit him not only against the Syrian-Greeks of Antiochus, but against the entire gentile world, which denied Jews the right to practice their faith as they saw fit. This echoes the prayer *Al HaNisim* (עַל הַנִּסִּים), "For the Miracles," which is inserted into the *Amidah* and *Birkat HaMazon* (Blessing after Meals) during Chanukah: "You delivered the mighty into the hands of the weak, the many into the hands of the few, the unclean into the hands of the pure, the evil into the hands of the righteous, and the arrogant into the hands of those who engage in your Torah."

2:68	Then Yochanan went out, that very	אָז יָצָא יוֹחָנָן בַּיּוֹם הַהוּא
2:69	day, and fought against the peoples,	וַיִּלָּחֶם בָּעַמִּים,
2:70	and inflicted a great slaughter upon them.	וַיַּהֲרֹג בָּהֶם הֶרֶג רָב.
2:71	The number of the dead whom	מִסְפַּר הַהֲרוּגִים אֲשֶׁר
2:72	he had slain that day was seven	הָרַג בַּיּוֹם הַהוּא שִׁבְעַת
2:73	thousand (one group was killing the	אֲלָפִים, אֲשֶׁר הָיוּ הוֹרְגִים אֵלֶּה
2:74	other).	לְאֵלֶּה.
2:75	Upon returning, he built a column in	בְּשׁוּבוֹ בָּנָה עַמּוּד
2:76	memorial, and he called it, "Maccabee,	עַל שְׁמוֹ, וַיִּקְרָא לוֹ: "מַכַּבִּי
2:77	Killer of the Strong."	מֵמִית הַחֲזָקִים".

***P'shat*: 2:68. Then Yochanan went out.** Yochanan not only exits the Temple precincts, thus escaping the vigilance and certain wrath of Nikanor's guards, he immediately again puts himself at risk in the service of God and the Jewish people as he goes out to battle. **2:69. the peoples.** Those peoples who came to persecute Judea and Jerusalem. The use of the plural here may indicate the varied ethnic composition of the Hellenistic world and, in particular, the many nationalities of the soldiers that fought beneath Antiochus's banner. **2:70. a great slaughter.** Yochanan's success in battle may be regarded as a sign of divine favor for his act of zealotry against Nikanor. **2:73–74. one group was killing the other.** This indicates that Yochanan is not alone. Rather, he inspires others to take up arms and fight their oppressors.

***D'rash*: 2:68. Yochanan went out.** The term יָצָא (*yatza*), "went out," is used technically in Rabbinic literature to indicate the fulfillment of a religious obligation. **2:70. a great slaughter.** This again echoes Judges 3:27–30, which reports the military victory of Israel over Moab wrought under Ehud's leadership after he smote Eglon. This victory put an end to Moab's domination of the Jewish people, "and the land had rest eighty years," that is, the people experienced not only political freedom, but a religious liberation. The Israelites no longer did that which was "evil in the eyes of God" (Judges 3:12). **2:76. Maccabee.** Though many modern scholars estimate this term to be one of uncertain origin and meaning, many assert that it means "hammer." This may be based upon *Mishnah B'chorot* 7:1, which includes in its list of those blemishes that disqualify a priest from officiating the מַקָּבָן (*makavan*), a man with a head the shape of a hammer. Scholar Solomon Zeitlin opines that Y'hudah, son of Mattathias, was known as "the Maccabee" because of the shape of his head.[12] At any rate, in this case, the term "Hammer" would be applied to Yochanan and his family for their strength and heroism. The Rabbis, however, see the word "Maccabee" as an acronym for the biblical phrase מִי כָמֹכָה בָּאֵלִם יְהֹוָה (*Mi chamochah ba-eilim Adonai*), "Who is like You, Eternal One among the gods that are worshiped" (Exodus 15:11). The verse comes from the Song at the Sea, which the Israelites sang in commemoration of God's victory over the Egyptians at the Reed Sea, an event that meant the rescue and continued survival of the escaped Hebrew slaves from the attack of the elite chariot brigades of the Egyptian army. Some claim that Mattathias and his sons emblazoned this phrase upon their shields. Some also suggest that the term "Maccabee" is an acronym for מַתִּתְיָהוּ כֹּהֵן בֶּן יוֹחָנָן (*Matityahu Kohein ben Yochanan*), "Mattathias the Priest, son of Yochanan," and hence identifies the family of brave liberators, under whose banner the Jews fought.

Zealotry in Judaism

The motifs of justice, courts of law, and rights to due process run throughout the five books of Judaism's sourcebook, the Torah. For example, the Book of Genesis hails the establishment of courts of law as one of the basic moral responsibilities of humanity, as their advent is considered to be one of the seven Noachide Laws incumbent upon all humanity.[13]

The Book of Exodus not only speaks of a progressive judicial system to ensure universal access to justice (Exodus 18:19–26), but also presents issues of law and justice as the essence of our covenant with God. This is evidenced by the fact that Scripture includes the prohibitions against murder, stealing, and bearing false witness as part of the Ten Statements divinely promulgated upon Mount Sinai (Exodus 20:13).

The Book of Leviticus firmly places matters of justice within the realm of holiness. The section commonly known as the Holiness Code states, "You shall not render an unfair decision: do not favor the poor or show deference to the rich; judge your kin fairly" (Leviticus 19:15).

The Book of Numbers depicts God commanding Moses to set aside cities of refuge where one who kills unintentionally may flee in order to escape the wrath of the blood avenger and to stand before a court of justice: "The cities shall serve you as a refuge from the avenger, so that killer may not die unless he has stood trial before the assembly" (Numbers 35:12).

Finally, the Book of Deuteronomy mainly consists of Moses's oratory to the Children of Israel during the final weeks of his life. The great prophet exhorts them to adopt those tenets that will facilitate their creation of a moral society in the Promised Land that will be a "light unto the nations."[14] Not surprisingly, Moses emphasizes justice: "You shall appoint magistrates and officials for your tribes, in all the settlements that the Eternal, your God is giving you, and they shall govern the people with due justice.... Justice, justice shall you pursue" (Deuteronomy 16:18, 20).

Amid this pervasive theme of orderly justice, the Torah relates the tale of Pinchas the son of Eleazar, the son of Aaron the priest: While the Children of Israel are camped in Shittim, a group of Moabite women seduce them, not only to illicit sexual encounter, but also to idolatry. In addition to the spiritual threat this represents to the young nation still wandering in the wilderness on their way to the Promised Land, a plague breaks out, annihilating no fewer than twenty-four thousand people. Among the sinners, Pinchas witnesses an Israelite prince and a Moabite princess publicly copulating. At this point, Pinchas takes it upon himself to thrust a spear through them both, effectively putting an end to the threat of both the spiritual and medical plagues (Numbers 25:1–9).

Far from plainly condemning Pinchas's zealotry as an act of summary justice, as one may have reason to expect, God grants him a "covenant of peace" and the hereditary High Priesthood (Numbers 25:12, 13). How can the same Torah that replaces the "hotness" of the blood avenger with the cool deliberation of the righteous judge, and the violence of vigilantism with the legal details of due process, not only countenance Pinchas's act, but reward him?

The answer is that legitimate zealotry obviously has a place within Judaism. But the Rabbis, understandably concerned with the spiritual and political consequences of legitimized violence, made certain that its place remains extremely narrow. While *Mishnah Sanhedrin* 9:6 includes, "If one has relations with a Cutite woman, zealots may kill him," the Rabbis of the Talmud explain that a zealous act may be condoned only under very specific conditions.

First, the act must not be personally motivated; that is, to be Jewishly legitimate, zealotry must be enacted solely for the benefit of God and the Jewish people. Secondly, the zealot must strike only while the perpetrator engages in the sin. If the sinner desists from the transgression and then the zealot strikes, the latter is guilty of murder and will be prosecuted in a court of law. In addition, the sinner may defend him- or herself from the zealot's pursuit. Third, the zealot's action must stem from an internal locus. No one is ever permitted to instruct another to engage in zealotry. Fourth, the act must not be the product of spur of the moment rage, but rather a clearly chosen path (Babylonian Talmud, *Sanhedrin* 82a).[15]

Despite Pinchas's zealotry meeting the above criteria, the Talmud (*Sanhedrin* 82b) teaches that there were Israelites who sought Pinchas's life. So Pinchas appealed to the ultimate Judge. He placed the bodies of the slain prince and princess before God and rhetorically asked if the lives of these two were worth the lives of twenty-four thousand. God agreed that Pinchas's act actually saved thousands of lives and granted him the divine covenant of peace, which spelled protection from those who would harm him. Thus, one may derive that zealotry may be used morally as a weapon against an extraordinary threat to the very existence of Judaism and the Jewish people.

The Talmud (*Sanhedrin* 82a) further emphasizes that this particular threat of the Moabite seduction could not have been met through the usual channels of jurisprudence. The text depicts Pinchas sitting in the court of law as the people's leaders, under orders from Moses, attempt to put a stop to the seduction and the plague by prosecuting the guilty parties. Seeing the ineffectual nature of legal due process in this context, Pinchas "got up from amid the assembly and took a spear in his hand" (Numbers 25:7).

According to the Talmud (*Sanhedrin* 82a), Pinchas hid the iron spearhead beneath his garment and used the long handle as a walking stick. He then pretended to seek illicit sexual contact for himself in order to gain access to the sinners, the prince and princess. Hence, we learn from Pinchas that deception may be employed for the sake of zealotry and that the rank and power of the targeted sinners should not interfere with an act of righteous zealotry.

In *M'gillat Antiochus*, Yochanan also meets the above Talmudic criteria for zealotry. Nikanor's bloody implementation of Antiochus IV's edicts constitutes an extraordinary threat to the very existence of the Jewish people, no less than the Moabite plague depicted in the Book of Numbers. Yochanan, like Pinchas before him, moved solely by the egregious evils of Nikanor's perpetration of mass murder and the desecration of the Temple, plans to take action. And just as Pinchas does not allow the high positions of the Israelite prince and Moabite princess to prevent him from his goal of saving the Jewish people, Yochanan remains undeterred by Nikanor's position of power as governor to interfere with his mission. Yochanan, like Pinchas, uses deception to gain private access to the governor. The fact that Yochanan offers a prayer to God before smiting Nikanor indicates not only the purity of his motive, but his clearheaded understanding of the moral issues at hand. According to our Torah and its Sages, human life is too precious to be taken without acknowledging the tragedy involved, even in self-defense. As we learn in *Pirkei Avot* 4:19, "Shmuel HaKatan says, 'Rejoice not when your enemy falls and let not your heart be glad when he stumbles.'"

It is this pervasive respect in Judaism for the sanctity of human life that has affected Rabbinic reaction to Pinchas's deed and zealotry in general to be far from universally positive. Our texts reveal discomfort about Pinchas and hence the role of zealotry. For instance, Rabbi Tzvi Y'hudah Berlin, in his commentary *Haamek Davar*, sees the divine covenant of peace as neither a guarantee of personal safety nor a reward for Pinchas. Rather, according to Berlin, the covenant of peace constitutes a protection from the zealous perpetrator's inner enemy; that is, the covenant of peace is a prescription to calm Pinchas down. Even the Psalmist cries out, "My zeal has consumed me!" (Psalm 119:139). In her *Studies in Bamidbar*, Nehama Leibowitz further points out that the Sages of the Jerusalem Talmud state that Pinchas's deed did not meet with the approval of Moses and the elders, the religious leaders of his time.[15]

One may surmise the Rabbi's transformation of Chanukah from what might have remained a Maccabean military victory celebration to a religious Festival of Lights has to do with their circumscribing and channeling the zealous impulse. As the *Union*

Prayer Book reminds us, "Light is the symbol of the divine."[16] Instead of striking out in violence for the sake of justice, Judaism, and the Jewish people, the Rabbis ordained that Jews strike up a symbolic light to share with the world. In lieu of violent overreaction, our religious authorities have prescribed that we use our zeal for right to spread the boons of spirituality, *chesed* (divine kindness), and morality, as represented by the lamps of Chanukah, which we display by our doors and in our windows for all to see. Thus may we fulfill Isaiah's prophecy that the Jewish people serve as a moral beacon unto the world, a "light to the nations" (Isaiah 42:6).

GLEANINGS

2:57–60 "He advanced three steps toward him, thrust the sword into his heart, and flung him mortally wounded into the holy court."

Religious Extremism

Probably no people on earth has suffered more from the evils of religious extremism than the Jews. Victims of crusades, jihads, inquisitions, pogroms, forced conversions, and expulsions, and in our own times the barbarism of modern state religion as well as bitter infighting within the Jewish community, Jews have learned to be wary of those who claim to act in the name of God.

> Ellen Frankel, *The Five Books of Miriam*, p. 233

Self-Defense in This World and the Next

"Assail the Midianites" (Numbers 25:17). Why? "For they assail you" (Numbers 25:18). From this the Sages have derived the maxim: If a man comes to kill you, kill him first. Rabbi Shimon says: How do we know that one who causes a man to sin is even worse than one who kills him? Because one who kills him does so only as regards this world but leaves him a share in the world-to-come. One who causes him to sin, however, kills him in this world and the next.

> *B'midbar Rabbah* 21:4

Zeal Against the Powerful

"The name of the Israelite man who was killed ... was Zimri son of Salu, chieftain of a Simeonite ancestral house" (Numbers 25:14). To make known the praiseworthiness of Pinchas, that although a prince was involved this did not prevent Pinchas from being zealous for the profanation of the name of God. That is why the verse reveals to you the name of the victim.

> Rashi on Numbers 25:14

Mattathias's Zeal

A Jewish man came forward in the sight of all to offer sacrifice upon the altar in Modi'in in accordance with the king's decree. When Mattathias saw this, he was filled with zeal and trembled with rage and let his anger rise, as was fitting he ran and slew him upon the altar. At the same time he also killed the king's official in charge of enforcing sacrifices, and he destroyed the altar. He acted zealously for the sake of the Torah, as Pinchas acted against Zimri the son of Salu. Mattathias cried out throughout the town in a loud voice, "All who are zealous for the sake of the Torah, who uphold the covenant, march out after me!"

> I Maccabees 2:23–27

Chapter 3

Creativity versus Rigidity: On Sabbath and Survival

In ancient days, as in our own times, a spectrum of movements and denominations existed within Judaism. One such denomination, called the Chasidim[1] or Pietists, believed that faith in God and strict adherence to God's commandments demanded that they rely only on divine providence for protection. As Antiochus decreed practice of the Sabbath and circumcision punishable by death, many Chasidim decided martyrdom to be the ultimate expression of Judaism.

On the other hand, the Maccabees developed a different, more flexible approach to Judaism. They believed that the Jews could not passively leave all of the issues related to their survival to God. Rather, human beings had to initiate action on their own behalf and needed to apply the laws and practices of Judaism creatively in order to meet the exigent demands of the age. The goal and consequence of such action and creativity would be the saving of Jewish life and the continuity of Judaism.

Ever since, Judaism has changed with and adapted to the particular needs of each generation. Of course, the pace, extent, and methods used to facilitate those changes constitute points of separation between the modern North American Jewish movements.[2] Generally, Reform Judaism may be regarded as the branch that most liberally countenances innovation to harmonize tradition and modernity in an effort to preserve the spirit and dynamism of the law, while at the same time maintaining a respect for personal autonomy.

3:1	So it was that when	וַיְהִי כַּאֲשֶׁר שָׁמַע
	Antiochus the king	אַנְטִיוֹכוֹס הַמֶּלֶךְ
3:2	heard that Nikanor, his governor, had been	כִּי נֶהֱרַג נִיקָנוֹר מִשְׁנֵהוּ,
3:3	killed, he was very distressed.	צַר לוֹ מְאֹד,
3:4	He dispatched (a messenger) to bring	וַיִּשְׁלַח לְהָבִיא לוֹ
	the evil Bagris to him,	אֶת בַּגְרִיס הָרָשָׁע

35

3:5	the deceiver of his people.	הַמַּטְעֶה אֶת עַמּוֹ.
3:6	Antiochus, the king, told	וַיַּעַן אַנְטִיוֹכוֹס הַמֶּלֶךְ וַיֹּאמֶר
3:7	Bagris, "Do you not know,	לְבַגְרִיס: "הֲלֹא יָדַעְתָּ
	have you not heard what the	אִם לֹא שָׁמַעְתָּ
3:8	Children of Israel have done to me?	אֲשֶׁר עָשׂוּ לִי בְּנֵי יִשְׂרָאֵל,
3:9	They have killed my soldiers and	הָרְגוּ חַיָּלַי,
3:10	plundered my camps and my officers. Now,	וַיָּבֹזּוּ מַחֲנוֹתַי וְשָׂרָי. עַתָּה
3:11	can you be sure of your wealth	עַל מָמוֹנְכֶם אַתֶּם בּוֹטְחִים,
	or that your	אוֹ עַל
3:12	homes are yours?	בָּתֵּיכֶם לָכֶם הֵם,
3:13	Come and let us go up against them,	בּוֹאוּ וְנַעֲלֶה עֲלֵיהֶם,
3:14	and we will abolish for them	וּנְבַטֵּל מֵהֶם
	the covenant that their God	הַבְּרִית
3:15	has established with them:	אֲשֶׁר כָּרַת לָהֶם אֱלֹהֵיהֶם:
3:16	Sabbath, New Moon, and circumcision."	שַׁבָּת, רֹאשׁ חֹדֶשׁ וּמִילָה".

***P'shat*: 3:5. the deceiver.** The Hebrew term הַמַּטְעֶה (*hamateh*) implies ''one who leads others astray,'' who causes them to err and sin. Bagris caused his people to sin by promoting the anti-Semitic lies he received from Antiochus, that the Jews constituted a threat to the economy of the region and the personal property of the non-Jewish population. **3:7–8. what the Children of Israel have done to me.** Initially, Antiochus does not cite any crime against the kingdom or the general population committed by the Jewish people; rather their self-defense is construed by the king as a personal insult. His main concern is obviously his own ego. **3:10. plundered my camps.** Antiochus's soldiers apparently camped in various spots in and around Jerusalem. **3:10. plundered my camps and my officers.** In order to arouse the complicity of his officers and perhaps to engender fear of his enemy, Antiochus casts Israel in the role of dangerous aggressors and thieves, despite the fact that he and his numerically and technologically superior forces initially attacked the Jews, causing them to defend themselves and fight for their survival. **3:10–11. Now, can you be sure of your wealth.** As a tactic to arouse the ire and military cooperation of his general Bagris and his soldiers against the Jews, Antiochus appeals to their personal fears. Thus, he feigns concern for the welfare of his pagan subjects. **3:14–15. the covenant that their God has established with them.** This again emphasizes not only the religious nature of Antiochus's war against the Jews, but his belief that their

36

enmity and their strength to resist lay in the Jews' devotion to God and Torah. As opposed to racial theories of anti-Semitism, this position supposes that Jews can be redeemed, that is, successfully assimilated into the Hellenistic world, once they are separated from their divine covenant.

D'rash: 3:4–5. the evil Bagris, the deceiver of his people. The Talmud associates arrogance with evil. Thus Rav states, "Arrogance is the equivalent of all the other sins" (Babylonian Talmud, *Sukkah* 29b). Thus, the midrash hints at Bagris's evil not only by his arrogance in naming a city after himself (see chapter 1), but for the crimes against humanity that he is about to commit. In addition to deceiving his people, the pagans of the Syrian-Greek world, by floating false fears to trick them into participating in an unjust war, he works feverishly to cause God's people Israel to sin by forsaking their divine covenant. *Pirkei Avot* 5:18 states that one who causes others to sin is so profligate that "no repentance will be possible." The prophet Micah (3:5–7) speaks of a class of false prophets who only care about enriching themselves and who bring magic (idolatrous) charms into Judah as "misleading" the people. Finally, I Maccabees 1:11 refers to the Jewish Hellenizers as "lawless men who misled many of their people." **3:10. plundered my camps and my officers.** Antiochus here speaks in consonance with many today who seek to characterize the State of Israel's efforts to defend itself against the ravages of several waves of organized attacks perpetrated upon it by various hostile governments and terrorist organizations as "aggression." **3:11. can you be sure of your wealth.** Antiochus plays upon the fears of the people to fuel his anti-Semitic rampage. The Nazis applied this same strategy in their propaganda, warning of some all-powerful, international Jewish conspiracy that controlled every bit of the world's wealth. In his opus *Mein Kampf*, Hitler referred to the Jew as an economic "parasite" whose monetary success and confidence would eventually render honest Aryan workers "propertyless in the truest sense of the word" and whose political influence would solidify his position as a "tyrant over peoples," making them "ripe for the slave's lot of permanent subjugation."[3]

3:17	Then the wicked Bagris and all his	אָז קָם בַּגְרִיס הָרָשָׁע
3:18	hosts rose up and invaded Jerusalem.	וְכָל מַחֲנוֹתָיו, וַיָּבוֹאוּ לִירוּשָׁלָיִם.
3:19	They perpetrated a great massacre	וַיַּהֲרֹג בָּהּ הֶרֶג רַב
3:20	and issued an absolute decree against	וַיִּגְזֹר בָּהּ גְּזֵרָה גְמוּרָה
3:21	Shabbat, Rosh Chodesh,	עַל שַׁבָּת, רֹאשׁ חֹדֶשׁ,
3:22	and circumcision. As a result of this,	וּמִילָה. בִּהְיוֹת זֶה,

3:23	the word of the king was	כַּאֲשֶׁר הָיָה דְּבַר הַמֶּלֶךְ
3:24	implemented with such alarming severity	נֶחְפָּז,
3:25	that when they found a man	מָצְאוּ אִישׁ
3:26	who circumcised his son,	אֲשֶׁר מָל בְּנוֹ,
3:27	they brought the man and his wife	וַיָּבִיאוּ הָאִישׁ וְאִשְׁתּוֹ,
3:28	and they hung them in front of	וַיִּתְלוּ אוֹתָם כְּנֶגֶד
3:29	the boy.	הַיֶּלֶד.

P'shat: 3:17–18. the wicked Bagris and all his hosts. I Maccabees 7:10 describes his hosts as "a large force." The force was so large that when Bagris sent messengers to the Maccabees with "peaceable but treacherous words," the latter realized that Bagris's intentions were violent because of the size of the force with which he came into the land of Judea. **3:20. absolute decree.** Although Antiochus previously issued a decree against Shabbat, Rosh Chodesh, and circumcision (see chapter 1), the "absoluteness" of this decree represents a zero-tolerance policy; that is, Bagris establishes and ruthlessly enforces the death penalty as punishment for violating the decree by observing the tenets of Judaism. **3:21. Shabbat, Rosh Chodesh.** According to II Maccabees 6:7, the Jews were forbidden to observe the biblical Sabbath, Rosh Chodesh, and the holy days of the Hebrew calendar as specified by the Torah, and the Syrian-Greeks forced them to participate in the monthly celebration of the king's birthday and the festival of Dionysus and to partake of their respective idolatrous sacrifices. **3:24. such alarming severity.** The Hebrew נֶחְפָּז (*nechpaz*) implies haste or alacrity. Bagris and his henchmen couldn't wait to implement the king's decree. **3:28–29. they hung them in front of the boy.** Despite the claim of the Hellenizers that Greek culture represented the epitome of sophisticated civilization, the panic of Bagris and his hosts to abrogate the laws of the Torah manifests itself in a frenzy of inhuman cruelty. Hence, the midrash reveals the moral bankruptcy of the Syrian-Greeks and the Hellenistic way of life.

D'rash: 3:18. rose up. This phrase echoes the Torah's description of the first murder: "Cain *rose up* against his brother Abel and killed him" (Genesis 4:8). The text here emphasizes that Cain and Abel were brothers, as is all humanity, since we hail from a single ancestor, Adam. As brothers and sisters, it behooves us to behave with love and kindness for one another, as opposed the hatred and cruelty wrought by Cain and by Bagris. **3:24. such alarming severity.** The use of the term נֶחְפָּז here echoes its use in Psalm 48:6, which describes the kings of the world assembling and attacking God's stronghold, the holy city of Jerusalem: "They saw and were amazed, they were terrified, they fled in haste [נֶחְפָּזוּ]." Thus, the term's appearance in the midrash hints that although Antiochus invaded and enforced his immoral, destructive decree with enthusiastic haste, it is with this same alacrity that he and the rest of the evildoers in the world will be repelled and scattered. This sense of frenzy or panic among the fleeing Syrian-Greeks conveyed by this term is again attested to by Deuteronomy 20:3, which depicts Moses informing the Children of Israel of the role of the priest in war. The priest shall address the people, "Hear, O Israel! You are about to join battle with your enemy. Let not your courage falter. Do not be in fear or in panic [וְאַל תַּחְפְּזוּ, *v'al tachp'zu*], or in dread of them." **3:28–29. they hung them in front of the boy.** This echoes the quintessential Rabbinic tale of martyrdom, that of Hannah and her seven sons. Chapter 7 of II Maccabees reports that the Syrian-Greeks bring Hannah and her sons before the king for their refusal to eat pork. The king tortures the sons to death one by one, compelling the mother and remaining sons to watch each murder.

3:30	And also, another woman	וְגַם אִשָּׁה
3:31	gave birth to a son	אֲשֶׁר יָלְדָה בֵּן
3:32	after the death of her husband,	אַחֲרֵי מוֹת בַּעְלָהּ,
3:33	circumcised him at eight days,	וַתָּמָל אוֹתוֹ לִשְׁמֹנַת יָמִים,
3:34	and went up upon the wall of Jerusalem	וַתַּעַל עַל חוֹמַת יְרוּשָׁלַיִם
3:35	with her circumcised son	וּבְנָהּ הַמָּהוּל
3:36	in her arms. She cried out	בְּיָדָהּ. וַתַּעַן
3:37	and said, "To you we say, wicked	וַתֹּאמַר: "לְךָ אוֹמְרִים, בַּגְרִיס
3:38	Bagris, you intend to tear	הָרָשָׁע, אַתֶּם חוֹשְׁבִים לְבַטֵּל
3:39	from us the covenant	מֵאִתָּנוּ הַבְּרִית
3:40	that God makes with us;	אֲשֶׁר כָּרַת עִמָּנוּ,
3:41	the covenant of our ancestors	בְּרִית אֲבוֹתֵינוּ
3:42	will not be torn from us,	לֹא נְבַטֵּל מִמֶּנּוּ
3:43	nor from our children's children."	וְלֹא מִבְּנֵי בָנֵינוּ."
3:44	She threw her son down to the	וַתַּפֵּל בְּנָהּ
3:45	ground and then herself after him,	לָאָרֶץ וַתִּפֹּל אַחֲרָיו,
3:46	and the two of them died as one.	וַיָּמוּתוּ שְׁנֵיהֶם כְּאֶחָד.
3:47	And many of the Children of Israel	וְרַבִּים מִבְּנֵי יִשְׂרָאֵל

3:48 would do the same in those days,	הָיוּ עוֹשִׂים כֵּן בַּיָּמִים הָהֵם,
3:49 but they would not change the	וְלֹא שִׁנּוּ
3:50 covenant of their ancestors.	בְּרִית אֲבוֹתָם.

P'shat: **3:31. gave birth to a son.** The fact that the birth of a son usually spells blessing and hope raises the reader's sense of positive expectation and provides pathos to the story of martyrdom that follows. **3:32. after the death of her husband.** That the woman gave birth to the husband's child after his death seems to imply that she is a war widow. Unlike the Torah's law that repeatedly points out the moral obligation not to afflict society's most vulnerable—a stranger, a widow, or an orphan (Exodus 22:20; Deuteronomy 24:17)—Bagris's cruelty wantonly victimizes everyone. **3:33. circumcised him at eight days.** Circumcision on the eighth day is in accordance with Jewish law: "In all your generations let every eight-day-old boy among you be circumcised" (Genesis 17:12). It is a sign of the covenant between God and the Jewish people. The fact that the mother performs the circumcision in the father's absence is especially praiseworthy, as according to the Talmud the obligation to circumcise devolves particularly upon the father.[4] **3:48. would do the same in those days.** They would rather sacrifice their lives for the sanctification of God's name than transgress the covenant.

D'rash: **3:33. circumcised him at eight days.** The mother circumcising her son parallels the heroic actions of Moses's wife, Zipporah, of whom the Torah reports "took a flint and cut off her son's foreskin" (Exodus 4:25). This oblique verse is understood by many to refer to Zipporah circumcising their son, thereby saving not only the life of the baby and Moses's life, but the mission of Israel in the world as well. **3:49–50. they would not change the covenant of their ancestors.** Change implies assimilation to Hellenistic ways. In fact, I Maccabees 1:49 sums up the object of Antiochus's decrees: "So that they might forget the Torah and change all of their religious ordinances." Despite the governmental demands applied by the Syrian-Greeks and social pressures from the society of Hellenized Jews to assimilate, the people stubbornly maintained their Jewish identities through the observance of mitzvot, particularly the covenant of circumcision, as attested to above. On the other hand, while the Jews refused to exchange the tenets of Torah for the laws of Hellenism, the fact that "they would not change" may also be understood as a tacit criticism of the Pietists, for they would not change their observance pattern. Ignoring the larger picture, the Pietists engendered a culture of martyrdom that threatened to destroy the Jewish people.

3:51	At that time, one group of the	בַּזְּמַן הַהוּא אָמְרוּ
3:52	Children of Israel said to the other,	בְּנֵי יִשְׂרָאֵל אֵלֶּה לָאֵלֶּה:
3:53	"Come, let us go and keep the Sabbath in a cave,	"בּוֹאוּ וְנֵלֵךְ וְנִשְׁבֹּת בִּמְעָרָה,
3:54	lest we desecrate	פֶּן נְחַלֵּל אֶת
3:55	the Sabbath day."	יוֹם הַשַּׁבָּת".
3:56	But they betrayed them to Bagris.	וַיַּלְשִׁינוּ אוֹתָם לִפְנֵי בַּגְרִיס.
3:57	Then Bagris sent armed men, who came and	אָז שָׁלַח בַּגְרִיס אֲנָשִׁים חֲלוּצִים, וַיָּבוֹאוּ
3:58	sat at the entrance to the cave and said,	וַיֵּשְׁבוּ עַל פִּי הַמְּעָרָה וַיֹּאמְרוּ:
3:59	"Children of Israel, come out	"בְּנֵי יִשְׂרָאֵל, צְאוּ
3:60	to us. Eat of our bread and drink of our	אֵלֵינוּ, אִכְלוּ מִלַּחְמֵנוּ וּשְׁתוּ
3:61	wine, and do as we do."	מִיֵּינֵנוּ, וּמַעֲשֵׂינוּ תִּהְיוּ עוֹשִׂים".
3:62	But, the Jews spoke up, one group	וַיַּעֲנוּ בְּנֵי יִשְׂרָאֵל
3:63	saying to the next, "We remember what	וַיֹּאמְרוּ אֵלֶּה לָאֵלֶּה "זוֹכְרִים אֲנַחְנוּ אֶת אֲשֶׁר
3:64	was commanded us on Mount Sinai:	נִצְטַוֵּינוּ עַל הַר סִינָי:
3:65	'Six days shall you labor and do all of	'שֵׁשֶׁת יָמִים תַּעֲבֹד וְעָשִׂיתָ כָּל מְלַאכְתֶּךָ,
3:66	your work, and the seventh day shall	וּבַיּוֹם הַשְּׁבִיעִי
3:67	you rest.' Now, it is better for us to die in the cave than	תִּשְׁבֹּת,' עַתָּה, טוֹב לָנוּ אֲשֶׁר נָמוּת בַּמְּעָרָה
3:68	to desecrate the Sabbath."	מֵאֲשֶׁר נְחַלֵּל אֶת יוֹם הַשַּׁבָּת".

P'shat: 3:51–52. one group of the Children of Israel. The response of the Chasidim, or Pietists, to the challenge of Hellenism is to rigidly adhere to traditional Jewish ways, as they understand them, even at the cost of their lives. **3:56. they betrayed them to Bagris.** The midrash does not specify exactly who betrays the Shabbat observers in the cave. It may be hostile gentiles who report the Jews to Bagris and his men. Or perhaps Hellenistic Jews who support the push toward assimilation betray the Shabbat observers—such is the magnitude of the threat of Hellenistic culture to the Jewish future. In fact, I Maccabees 1:11 refers to the Jewish Hellenizers as "lawless" men, those who had thrown off the yoke of the Torah and the covenant it represents, and depicts them attempting to persuade the rest of Jewry over to their position:

"Let us go and make a covenant with the nations around us, for ever since the time we became separated from the nations, many misfortunes have overtaken us." **3:56. betrayed.** The Hebrew וַיַּלְשִׁינוּ (*vayalshinu*) implies that they "inform" upon or "slander" the Shabbat observers. **3:60–61. Eat of our bread and drink of our wine, and do as we do.** By imploring the Jews to partake of nonkosher food, the Syrian-Greeks again imply that there is nothing inherently incorrigible in the Jews themselves; rather their problem resides in their stubborn insistence upon their right to remain religiously distinct. Assimilation of the Jews would spell Greek victory. **3:60–61. Eat of our bread and drink of our wine.** Since bread and wine are traditionally used to welcome Shabbat, their mention by the Syrian-Greek soldiers may be considered sardonic and taunting. **3:64. Mount Sinai.** Mount Sinai is remembered as the site of revelation of the Decalogue. According to tradition, God established a covenant with the entire Jewish people there. The Tablets of Testimony bear witness to the covenant. Upon them is written, "Six days you shall labor and do all your work, but the seventh day is a Sabbath of the Eternal your God" (Exodus 20:9–10; Deuteronomy 5:13–14).

D'rash: **3:56. betrayed.** A derivative of this term (וַיַּלְשִׁינוּ, *vayalshinu*) is found in the traditional version of the daily *Amidah*, the central, "standing" prayer of the Jewish worship service: "And may the slanderers [וְלַמַּלְשִׁינִים, *v'lamalshinim*] have no hope, and may all evil perish instantly."[5] As in the case of the midrash, exactly who "the slanderers" are remains a question. I Maccabees 1:11–15 does, however, point to the existence of Hellenizers within the Jewish camp. These militant assimilationists aligned themselves with the king, built a gymnasium (Greek cultural center) in Jerusalem, and even surgically removed the marks of their circumcision. It is not difficult to imagine that these assimilationists would inform the authorities about Jews flouting the king's edict by observing the traditional Shabbat in a cave. **3:58. cave.** The Bible and the midrash relate both negative and positive associations with caves. On the positive side, caves can provide protection. For instance, the midrash *Maaseh Avraham Avinu* depicts the baby Abraham as being sheltered in a cave from the murderous rampage of King Nimrod. In the Torah (Exodus 33:22) God places Moses in a "cleft of a rock" to protect him from the intensity of the Divine Presence. The Talmud (*M'gillah* 19b) interprets a "cleft of a rock" to have been a cave. In I Kings 19:9, Elijah the prophet seeks shelter in a cave from the evil intentions of Queen Jezebel. The Talmud (*Shabbat* 33b–34a) teaches that Shimon bar Yochai successfully hid in a cave from the wrath of the Romans for twelve years. Caves may also be seen in a negative light. The midrash's inclusion of the Pietists who go to the cave to observe Shabbat may be seen as a polemic against those who seek to isolate themselves in order to observe Judaism. Like the Essenes of the Dead Sea caves, these Shabbat observers handicap themselves by their removal from the commerce of the general community. The Talmud indicates that Rabbi Shimon bar Yochai emerged from the cave in which he had isolated himself tainted by his experience (Talmud, *Shabbat* 33b). Upon seeing people engaged in daily activities, such as plowing fields and sowing seeds, he became filled with such disgust and hostility that whatever he gazed upon was immediately consumed by the fire of his eyes. The Jewish ideal is one of holiness achieved among others. **3:58. cave.** I Maccabees 2:29–38 informs that those who had "gone down to the hiding places in the wilderness" refused to fight on Shabbat. The text contrasts their passive resistance ("they did not answer them or hurl a stone at them or block up their hiding places") with Mattathias's ruling: "Let us fight against anyone who comes to attack us on the Sabbath day; let us not all die as our kindred did in their hiding places." **3:60–61. Eat of our bread and drink of our wine.** Bread and wine bear special religious significance. This may be evidenced from the mention in Genesis of Malchizedek, "priest of God Most High," bringing out bread and wine to preside over a religious ritual blessing of Abraham and thanking God for assisting the patriarch in battle and allowing him to rescue his nephew, Lot (Genesis 14:18–20). The special religious nature of bread and wine is further attested to by the fact that they are the only two items of food or drink assigned specific blessings in Jewish tradition. As alluded to above, Jews use bread and wine ritually to welcome Shabbat. **3:60. Eat of our bread.** The Talmud (*Shabbat* 17b) records the decision of the Rabbis to forbid *pat acum* (פַּת עַכּוּ"ם) "the bread of idolators," as a measure to prevent unhealthy intercourse, social and sexual, that could lead to the practice of idolatry among Jews. The prohibition is one of the Eighteen Enactments made by the disciples of Beit Shammai and Beit Hillel in order to maintain spiritual purity in Israel. **3:60–61. and drink of our wine.** The wine of the Syrian-Greeks falls under a special category of dietary law, that of *yein nesech* (יֵין נֶסֶךְ), "wine of idolatrous libation." Maimonides lists this prohibition as one of the commandments of the Torah based upon the following verse, which appears in the Song of Moses, describing the sins of the people's encounter with idolatry: "Who ate the fat of their offerings and drank their libation wine" (Deuteronomy 32:38). Drinking the wine of the Syrian-Greeks would then be tantamount to committing idolatry. **3:61. do as we do.** Since the midrash depicts the armed men making this demand with the threat of violence and death, we may understand the text to teach that the Greeks stressed assimilation as the Jew's best chance for survival. **3:67–68. better for us to die than to desecrate the Sabbath.** The actions of the Maccabees, as well as normative Jewish law, contradict this statement. I Maccabees 2:40–41 depicts Mattathias and his friends reasoning, "If we all do as our brothers have done and do not fight against the gentiles [on the Sabbath] for our lives and our laws, they will now quickly wipe us off the face of the earth." On that day they came to a decision: "If any man comes against us in battle on the Sabbath day, we shall fight against him, and let us not all die as our brothers died in their hiding places." According to the Rabbis, the words of Leviticus 18:5, "You shall keep My laws and My rules, by the pursuit of which human beings shall live," teach specifically "you shall live by them (the commandments)," not die by them (Talmud, *Yoma* 85b). Therefore, the saving of a life takes precedence over the vast majority of other mitzvot, including Sabbath observance.[6]

3:69	At this, since the Jews did not	בִּהְיוֹת זֶה כַּאֲשֶׁר לֹא
3:70	go out to them,	יָצְאוּ אֲלֵיהֶם הַיְּהוּדִים,
3:71	they brought trees	וַיָּבִיאוּ עֵצִים
	and set them afire at the mouth of the cave.	וַיִּשְׂרְפוּ עַל פִּי הַמְּעָרָה,
3:72	About a thousand men and women	וַיָּמוּתוּ כְּאֶלֶף אִישׁ וְאִשָּׁה.
3:73	died.	
3:74	After this, the five	אַחֲרֵי כֵן יָצְאוּ
	sons of Mattathias,	חֲמֵשֶׁת בְּנֵי מַתִּתְיָה,
3:75	Yochanan and his four brothers,	יוֹחָנָן וְאַרְבַּעַת אֶחָיו,
3:76	went out and fought against the peoples,	וַיִּלָּחֲמוּ בָעַמִּים,
3:77	and effected a great slaughter.	וַיַּהַרְגוּ בָהֶם הֶרֶג רָב,
3:78	They drove them to the islands of the sea,	וַיְגָרְשׁוּם לְאִיֵּי הַיָּם,
3:79	for they trusted in the God of the	כִּי בָטְחוּ בֵּאלֹהֵי
3:80	heavens.	הַשָּׁמָיִם.

***P'shat*: 3:76. went out and fought.** The Maccabees actively battle Antiochus's forces, in contradistinction to the passivity of the Pietist cave observers. **3:76. the peoples.** The Maccabees fight against the army of Bagris, which is composed of soldiers of various nationalities. **3:78. they drove them.** Yochanan and his four brothers drive Bagris and the Syrian-Greeks from the Land of Israel, indicating divine favor with their decision to actively resist. **3:78. islands of the sea.** The islands of the sea may be considered a metaphor for the farthest reaches of the world and the depths of exile. **3:79. they trusted.** The sons of Mattathias gain strength and score their victory as a result of their faith in God.

D'rash: **3:76. went out and fought.** The Hebrew יָצְאוּ (*yatzu*), used to express "they went out," as mentioned above (see comment to 2:64), is a technical term used in Rabbinic literature to mean that one has fulfilled a religious commandment. The midrash, then, describes the Maccabees as "going out" and fulfilling their religious obligations by their active approach to Judaism's survival. As opposed to this, the text informs us that the Pietists, by their passive approach, "did not go out," (3:69–70), implying that their passive martyrdom did not meet the religious requirements of the day. **3:78. islands of the sea.** Isaiah 11:11 alludes to the advent of the messianic age when "God will set a hand again the second time to recover the remnant of God's people, that shall remain from Assyria, and from Egypt, and from Pathros, and from Cush, and from Elam, and from Shinar, and from Hamath, and from the islands of the sea." So we may understand that while the prophet depicts God rescuing God's penitent people from the "islands of the sea" and gathering them for a righteous future, the midrash pictures God's hand, as it were, thrusting Bagris and his evil henchmen out to the islands of the sea as a consequence of their evil. **3:79–80. for they trusted in the God of the heavens.** The mention of the God of the heavens at this point implies that the victory did not solely belong to the Maccabees. Rather, God, who is the Master of the universe, wrought divine redemption through God's human agents. This is conceptually similar to the attribution of the Exodus from Egypt to God, who worked through God's servant Moses. The statement also serves to legitimize the leadership and actions of the Hasmoneans, as not only did they trust in the God of the heavens, but their incredible victory against a much stronger and larger fighting force would indicate that the God of the heavens trusted in them.

The Chasidim, or Pietists

The midrash relating the incident of martyrdom at the cave on Shabbat alludes to a group of pedantic religious observers commonly known as the Chasidim (חֲסִידִים), or Pietists. These terms refer to an ancient group that should not be confused with the modern-day Chasidim. The Greek term for them, Hasideans or Asideans, or *Asidaioi* to be more exact, is a Hellenization of the Hebrew term *Chasidim*.

Scant information concerning the Pietists remains. I Maccabees 2:42 constitutes the first mention of the Pietists by name, indicating that following the Shabbat massacre at the cave (a scene incorporated into *M'gillat Antiochus*) a "group of Pietists" joined the Maccabean rebellion—"mighty warriors of Israel, all who volunteered in defense of the Torah." The fact that the text offers no further explanation of just who the Pietists were would indicate that the group needed no introduction or explanation, for it was well-known. Jonathan A. Goldstein, in his commentary to I Maccabees, argues the Pietists to have been a "well-defined group among the Jews."[7]

Goldstein also suggests that although outsiders may have referred to them as Pietists, the group may have called themselves "Seekers of Justice and Vindication," after Zephaniah 2:3: "Seek the Eternal, all you humble of the earth who have performed God's judgment. Seek righteousness, seek humility! Perhaps you will be concealed in the day of the Eternal's wrath."[8]

This moniker, of course, would fit in with I Maccabees' depiction of the Pietists' initial reluctance to take up arms against Antiochus's regime and refusal to even defend their lives on Shabbat. They may have thought of themselves as "the humble of the earth," those who unquestioningly accept the rule of gentile kings as God's judgment and will. As seekers of righteousness, the Pietists would be scrupulous in their mitzvah performance so that they would be divinely protected during any period of persecution, "the day of the Eternal's wrath."

According to scholar Lawrence H. Schiffman, the Pietists constituted a "loosely organized sect" of unknown origin who resided in ancient Judea. They remained active throughout the Maccabean age and, in his opinion, into the time of the Mishnah, about the year 200 C.E.[9] Professor Victor Tcherikover, however, argues that the Pietists emerged from the society of scribes that existed in the early second century B.C.E. to become chief among them. The people knew the Pietists well and regarded them as the authoritative interpreters of the regulations and commandments of the Torah.

Tcherikover also opines that although initially the Pietists refused to fight on Shabbat, considering them conscientious pacifists or "harmless and peaceful people" would be a mistake. The fact that the Pietists joined the Maccabees "immediately after Mattathias raised the standard of rebellion" indicates that they had organized themselves into a fighting community in the cause of national resistance.[10] The reference in I Maccabees 2:42 to the Pietists as "mighty warriors in Israel" would seem to support Tcherikover's contention.

I Maccabees 7:13 reports that in the year 151 B.C.E., after the religious phase of the struggle had been won, as marked by the Temple's rededication and the resumption of the sacrificial cult, the Pietists broke ranks with Y'hudah Maccabee and his followers. But the eventual denouement of the Pietists remains a matter of scholarly debate. Some promote the idea that the Pietists developed into the Essenes, a group of ascetics who withdrew to caves in an effort to observe the Torah properly apart from what they saw as the corruption of the religious and political life of Jerusalem. These scholars look to the description of the Pietists presented in I Maccabees as "those who went into the wilderness" to support their view. But the Pietists of I Maccabees may have receded into the wilderness only as a consequence of Antiochus's oppression and subsequent war, not necessarily to reside there permanently as a way of expressing their distress with the religio-political scene of Jerusalem.

Other scholars regard the Pietists as the spiritual antecedents to the Pharisees, the proto-Rabbis, the architects of modern Rabbinic Judaism. Proponents of this position look to the detailed religious observance common to both groups as well as the use of the word *chasid* (חָסִיד, "pious one") in Rabbinic literature to support their view. But the word can simply mean one who is saintly, not necessarily a member of the ancient Judean Pietist group of the Maccabean era.

Whatever eventually happened to the Pietist group depicted in the midrash, one fact remains certain: those Pietists had no connection with any of the later groups or movements of the same name. In particular, one should not confuse the Pietists of the midrash with the Chasidei Ashkenaz of medieval Germany nor the modern-day Chasidic movement. While the ancient Pietists lived in Judea and practiced a rigid ritualistic life, the Chasidei Ashkenaz developed in twelfth-century Germany around the idea that Judaism's ultimate expression resides in acts of moral purity. Judah ben Samuel of Regensburg (d. 1217) and his disciple, Eleazar ben Judah of Worms (d. 1238), served as leaders of the movement. *Sefer HaChasidim* (Book of the Pious) presents the bulk of their teachings. It urges adherents to achieve true piety by going beyond the letter of the law in matters of humility, asceticism, and moral and ethical practices.

Israel ben Eliezer, the Baal Shem Tov (Master of the Good Name; 1699–1761), founded the modern-day Chasidic movement in southern Poland and the Ukraine during the eighteenth century. Following the Chmelnitzki massacres that destroyed many practitioners and centers of Torah scholarship and the disappointment of Shabbetai Zvi's false messiahship, the Besht (acronym for Baal Shem Tov) emphasized the joy of religious experience and true faith as a means of divine connection over scholarly learning, which was not available to the masses at the time. The movement quickly spread across Eastern Europe and eventually came to embrace Kabbalah, Jewish mysticism, and to be centered on certain rebbes[11] or religious leaders. These rebbes most often handed the reigns of leadership to other family members, forming Chasidic dynasties. Many of these leaders brought their followers from their Eastern European towns of origin to the United States, but still called their group by the towns from which they hailed. They also maintained the same clothing they wore in Europe, which by now has become sort of a Chasidic uniform. The modern Chasidim adopted their raiment from the medieval noblemen of Eastern Europe, and it bears no resemblance to the outfits worn by the residents of ancient Judea.

Heroines and Chanukah

Jewish tradition recognizes the role of women regarding the Chanukah miracle and its observance. In the words of Rabbi Y'hoshua ben Levi, "Women are obligated in the mitzvah of kindling the Chanukah light, for they too were part of that miracle" (Babylonian Talmud, *Shabbat* 23a). Rashi there alludes to their oppression by and rescue from the Greek practice of "first-night privileges," the policy of forcing every Jewish virgin bride to first submit to the local Greek magistrate on her wedding night. Rashi also states, "Through the hand of a woman was the miracle wrought."

The *Shulchan Aruch* suggests that in honor of the role of women in the Chanukah victory, women should refrain from working during the holiday for at least as long as the candles burn (*Orach Chayim, Hilchot Chanukah* 670:1). Moses Isserles, in his gloss to *Orach Chayim* 670:2, says the custom of eating dairy on Chanukah is "because the miracle occurred through milk that Judith fed the enemy." This echoes Yael's defeat of the Canaanite general Sisera, as depicted in chapters 4–5 of the Book of Judges. Like Judith, Yael renders unconscious an enemy who threatens to annihilate the Jewish people by feeding him dairy. Once asleep, she drives a stake through his temple. This fulfills the prediction of Deborah, the prophetess and leader of the Jewish people at that time, "The Eternal will give Sisera over into the hand of a woman" (Judges 4:9).

Solomon Ganzfried, in his *Kitzur Shulchan Aruch*, clarifies the *Shulchan Aruch* and Isserles's gloss. Ganzfried cites the custom of women refraining from work while the Chanukah candles burn to remember both the harsh decree of first-night privileges and the miracle effected by "a very beautiful woman," the daughter of Yochanan the High Priest.[12] When the monarch demanded she lay with him, she replied in the affirmative. Yochanan's daughter then fed him cheese, which made him thirsty, followed by intoxicating wine. She severed his head and brought it back to Jerusalem. When the enemy general saw the king's head, he and his army miraculously fled.

Some Sephardic communities, particularly those in North Africa (Algeria, Libya, Tunisia, and Morocco), dedicate the seventh night of Chanukah to Jewish women, declaring it Chag HaBanot, the Festival of Daughters. The seventh night of the Festival of Lights holds a special significance for women, as it is also Rosh Chodesh Tevet, the New Moon of Tevet.

Chag HaBanot recalls and celebrates the heroic role of women in the Chanukah story through a variety of customs. Women share a feast that includes cheese, recalling Judith (or, according to Ganzfried, Yochanan, the High Priest's daughter) saving the Jewish people through the agencies of cheese and wine to render the enemy leader unconscious. Sometimes, women gather in the synagogue on Chag HaBanot, touch the Torah, and pray for the health of their daughters. Girls who are fighting are expected to reconcile on this night. Mothers give gifts to their daughters. Bridegrooms provide gifts for their brides. Older and younger women join together in dance. Grandmothers and mothers pass down family heirlooms. All of these traditions celebrate an active, life-affirming approach by women towards Chanukah, Jewish continuity, and improving the world.

While *M'gillat Antiochus* presents the widow who heroically circumcises her son in defiance of Antiochus's edict and Bagris's ruthless enforcement of it, she ultimately gives herself over to martyrdom. She stands upon the Jerusalem city wall, throws her baby down, and then jumps off the wall, "and the two of them died as one" (3:46). The fact that many of the Children of Israel had adopted similar forms of resistance, variations on the theme of martyrdom, provides rationale and motivation for the Maccabees to pursue a different course of action to ensure Jewish survival.

Jewish tradition does, however, provide alternative visions of heroism among women connected with the story of Chanukah. The respective tales of Judith, daughter of Merari, and Hannah, the daughter of Mattathias, provide active models of heroic resistance. Many Jews have retold and continue to tell and celebrate these stories as part of their Chanukah festivities.

The Apocryphal Book of Judith, probably written sometime during the Second Temple period,[13] features as the title character a young widow, well-connected, wealthy, and devoted to God and her late husband, who courageously and actively engages in the effort to save the Jewish people "against all odds." Her name, Judith, יְהוּדִית (*y'hudit*), means "Jewess," implying that she is the ideal Jewish woman.

The story pits Judith against Holofernes, an Assyrian general appointed by King Nebuchadnezzar to attack Jerusalem, destroy the Temple, and carry away its holy vessels of gold and silver. In order to get to Jerusalem, Holofernes must first go through a small town nestled in a narrow mountain pass called Bethulia.

Holofernes arrives with a great host and besieges Bethulia. The ranking male authorities, including the High Priest in Jerusalem, instruct the people of Bethulia to pray. But after the siege goes on for thirty-four days, the authorities advise the people to surrender and thus give themselves over to slavery.

Judith, however, formulates a plan. One evening she manages to escape the town and tells the Assyrians that she has some valuable intelligence to relate to the general. They take her to Holofernes's tent. Her intelligence stimulates his interest, and her beauty arouses his lust. On her third night in Holofernes's camp, the general throws a large drinking party. Judith guides him to the consumption of a prodigious quantity of wine. While Holofernes remains in a stupor, Judith unsheathes a sword, prays to God for strength, and cuts off the head of the oppressor.

She carries Holofernes's head back to Bethulia to publicize the miracle of her victory and to rally others to fight for the cause of Jewish survival. They heed her advice. The Jews take up arms, attack the Assyrians, and rout them. An era of peace and adherence to the covenant ensues.

The Book of Judith, an obvious work of fiction,[14] demonstrates many parallels with the story of Chanukah. Like the Maccabees, Judith must not only battle a foreign enemy,[15] with designs against the Temple and Judaism, but she must also rally other Jews to her cause. She must convince them that taking an active approach is an example of covenantal behavior. Going up against Holofernes and his host, Judith is obviously greatly outnumbered, but with personal fortitude and God's help she proves successful. She needs to save Jerusalem, the Temple, and the Jewish people. Like the Book of Judith, the battles of the Maccabees against the Syrian-Greeks pit the few against the many. Our midrash teaches us that with personal courage and God's help, they also successfully push the oppressors out of Jerusalem and not only save the Temple, but champion God's covenant with Israel and ensure the future of the Jewish people.

The second of these stories, the legend of Hannah, the daughter of Mattathias the priest, is found in a medieval midrash probably composed in tenth- or eleventh-century Europe.[16] The midrash depicts a time when the Greeks are plotting, "Come let us invent harsh new decrees that will cause the Jews to reject their God and believe in our gods."

First, they decree that all Jews who have a door must write upon it, "Israel has no relationship to the God of Israel." This forces the Jews to rid themselves of doors. Without doors there can be no privacy. Jews can no longer eat or drink or sleep with their spouses in dignity. Without doors, anyone can come in or out at will. The Jews live in fear.

But the Jews persevere. In retaliation, the Greeks promulgate another decree: "Every man is forbidden to let his wife go to the *mikveh*,[17] under punishment of death." Since a woman was required to visit a *mikveh* after menstruation before resuming sexual relations with her husband, this decree represents a significant hardship as well as a form of population control. Rather than go against Jewish law, Jewish couples decide to avoid intercourse without ritual immersion by separating from their spouses completely.

Since the Jews manage to endure even this second decree, the Greeks legislate an even more bitter rule, that of "first-night privileges." As noted above, they mandate that every Jewish bride go directly from her marriage celebration to the local Greek official to have sexual relations with him for the first night and only then return to her husband. When the Jews hear this decree, they begin to desist from marriage, preferring to grow old as virgins. Three years and eight months after the decree goes into effect, Hannah, the daughter of Mattathias the priest, marries. All the great personages of Israel attend and celebrate. As they sit down to eat, Hannah rises from her bridal chair, claps her hands as a gesture of mourning, and tears off her bridal wreath and the rest of her clothing. She stands exposed before all Israel, her father, her mother, her bridegroom, and her five brothers.

When the five brothers see her, they feel embarrassed, ashamed, and then angry. They declare, "Take her out and burn her,"[18] for she dared appear naked in public.

Hannah then accuses those who would judge her, "If you are so zealous over appearing naked before this righteous audience—though I did not sin sexually—then why aren't you zealous about my purity when you yourselves are handing me over to be exploited by this uncircumcised Greek?"

Hannah then prays to God for strength. Her prayer and her accusations galvanize Y'hudah and his four brothers to action. Hannah and her brothers and a host of other Jews then march up to the home of the Greek magistrate, who in his hubris assumes the Jews have come to celebrate his "first-night privileges." The Jewish force led by the Maccabees cuts off the magistrate's head and rout the soldiers in his camp.

The story ends with a voice from heaven: "The lamb, which went forth to do battle with Antiochus, has been victorious," and the assurance that this victory resulted in *t'shuvah*, Torah, and righteous deeds.

As with Judith, Hannah's heroism resides not only in her courage to personally stand up against victimization, but in her talent to rally other Jews to her cause and course of action. In fact, this medieval midrash lauds Hannah as the one who galvanizes her father and her brothers, the Maccabees, to begin the revolt against Antiochus and his destructive decrees. Thus, Hannah's actions ultimately spell religious freedom and continuity for the Jewish people.

Both the story of Judith and that of Hannah teach valuable lessons for today's world. They testify to the reality that gender need not be the determinant of greatness. Rather, courage, the strength of faith, and the willingness to take action ensure Judith and Hannah's success and ours. In both these stories women oppose injustice, not only by forming a domestic support system for the fighters, but by themselves taking action. In doing so, they personally work to defeat evil, as well as inspire others to join the continuing struggle for good.

These stories imply that not only can women perform successfully and even heroically in the public sphere, but women can also excel as leaders. This reality impelled the Reform Movement to become the first stream of Judaism to ordain women as rabbis in 1972. This move proved to be part of a general ethical trend to empower women in religious affairs, as Reform's Centenary Perspective of 1976 asserts, "women should have full rights to practice Judaism."[19] In the words of Rabbi Eugene Borowitz, "Reform Judaism has since the early nineteenth century called for the equality of women in modern Jewish life."[20]

In addition to supporting women's rights, the stories of Hannah and Judith may also inspire an expansion of our own Chanukah celebrations. Rabbi Jill Hammer recommends that we incorporate aspects of the North African Chag HaBanot, the Festival of the Daughters, into our own Chanukah observance. Rabbi Hammer suggests that on the seventh night of the Festival of Lights we hold a special candlelighting ceremony dedicated to Judith and other Jewish heroes. Perhaps each candle of the *chanukiyah* can be lit in honor of a different admirable Jewish woman: heroes, teachers, leaders, or beloved family members. After the candlelighting, one may serve a special Chanukah dairy dish, in commemoration of Judith's victory, and then pass down a gift of family, personal, or spiritual significance. One can also celebrate the Festival of Daughters as a time of healing prayer: "May the One who blessed Sarah, Rivkah, Rachel, and Leah, bless and heal (insert names) and grant them vitality and courage. May they be strengthened as the heroes of Chanukah were strengthened. May they be granted the boldness of Judah, the fierce love of Hannah, and the wisdom and bravery of Judith. Send blessing on all the works of their hands, and show them kindness, peace, justice, and compassion. Amen."[21]

May these stories of courage and heroism continue to inspire all of us to dedicate ourselves anew to the goal of reaching our highest potentials as God's partners in making this world a more moral and holy place. And may the memories of the deeds of our ancestors expand and enhance our observance of the Festival of Lights.

GLEANINGS

3:9–12 "They have killed my soldiers and plundered my camps and officers. Now, can you be sure of your wealth or that your homes are yours?"

An Egregious Forgery

We have limitless ambitions, inexhaustible greed, merciless vengeance, and hatred beyond imagination. We are a secret army whose plans are impossible to understand by using honest methods. Cunning is our approach, mystery our way.

The Protocols of the Elders of Zion, cited in Abraham H. Foxman, *Never Again? The Threat of the New Anti-Semitism*, p. 215

3:30–33 "A woman gave birth to a son . . . circumcised him"

In Full Voice

I remember signing up for a course in 1980 entitled "Feminist Jewish Theology" taught by Dr. Judith Plaskow. I was incredulous that those words could be used together. What was so amazing? I think it was the willingness of women to say "We are worthy to share our images of God in full voice. We are also created in God's image."

Rabbi Sheila Peltz Weinberg, in *Lifecycles: Jewish Women on Life Passages & Personal Milestones*, vol. 1, ed. Debra Orenstein, p. 385

3:30–33, 41–43 "A woman gave birth to a son . . . circumcised him. . . . 'The covenant of our ancestors will not be torn from us, nor from our children's children.'"

An Ancient Understanding

To witness a *Brit Milah* is to experience a primitive enactment of a very ancient understanding that this child belongs not only to his parents, but also to God—and

God wants what parents cannot fully understand. Through the *Brit Milah*, the child is wrested from his parents to fulfill the ancient demand. . . . Not only does the boy emerge physically different after the *Brit Milah*, but he is also transformed from baby to covenanted Jew; from an infant with no history, to a person with a past and a future.

Rabbi Laura Geller, in *Lifecycles: Jewish Women on Life Passages & Personal Milestones*, vol. 1, ed. Debra Orenstein, pp. 58, 59

3:41–43 "The covenant of our ancestors will not be torn from us"

Social Injustice

At the age of eight I used to dream of becoming a Judith and visioned myself in the act of cutting off Holofernes' head to avenge the wrongs of my people. But since I had become aware that social injustice is not confined to my own race, I had decided that there were too many heads for one Judith to cut off.

Emma Goldman, *Living My Life* (Knopf, 1931), quoted in Ellen Jaffe-Gill, ed., *The Jewish Woman's Book of Wisdom*, p. 90

3:56 "they betrayed [slandered, informed upon] them"

The Power of the Tongue

"Death and life are in the power of the tongue" (Proverbs 18:21). Everything depends upon the tongue. It can merit life, or bring guilt upon itself and bring death. If a man employs his tongue to learn Torah and to please the Eternal, he acquires everlasting life. If he uses it to carry slanders and to speak evil, he earns death in the world-to-come.

Tanchuma Buber to *M'tzora*, chapter 2

3:60–61 "Eat of our bread and drink of our wine, and do as we do."

Keeping Kosher

[Keeping kosher was] the symbol of an initiation, like the insignia of a secret brotherhood, that set her apart and gave her freedom and dignity. Every law whose yoke she accepted willingly seemed to add to her freedom: she herself had chosen ... to enter that brotherhood. Her Judaism was no longer a stigma, a meaningless accident of birth from which she could escape.... It had become a distinction, the essence of her self-hood, what she was, what she wanted to be, not merely what she happened to be.

Jessie Sampter, *In the Beginning* (unpublished novel), quoted in Elaine Bernstein Partnow, ed., *The Quotable Jewish Woman*, p. 220

Yayin Nesech

The wine of idolaters is forbidden, and the prohibition subsumes even the derivation of benefit, as it is written: "the wine of whose libations they drank" (Deuteronomy 32:38). Just as benefit may not be derived from their sacrifices, so it may not be derived from their wine.

Babylonian Talmud, *Avodah Zarah* 29b

3:67–68 "better for us to die than to desecrate the Sabbath"

Yom Kippur: The Sabbath of Sabbaths

The great scholar Rabbi Hayyim Soloveitchik was known for being lenient about allowing very sick people to eat on the fast of Yom Kippur. When asked to explain why, Reb Hayyim answered: "I am not at all lenient about eating on Yom Kippur. I am just very strict in cases of *pikuach nefesh* [where life is at stake]."

Joseph Telushkin, *Jewish Literacy*, p. 521

The Big Picture

Rabbi Shimon ben Menasya said: "A man may profane one Sabbath in order that he may observe many Sabbaths."

Talmud, *Yoma* 85b

3:76 "fought against the peoples"

Which a Man Shall Do

Rabbi Meir used to say: Whence is it derived that even a gentile who occupies himself with Torah is like the High Priest? From: "which a man shall do" [Leviticus 18:5, "You shall keep My laws and My rules, which a man shall do, and he shall live in them: I am the Eternal"]. It is not written: "priests, Levites, or Israelites," but "a man." This teaches us that even a gentile who occupies himself with Torah is like the High Priest.

Babylonian Talmud, *Bava Kama* 38a

Chapter 4

Earthly (Tyrannical) Power versus Divine Omnipotence: Preparing for Confrontation

This chapter again illustrates a fundamental disparity in approach to life and outlook between the Syrian-Greeks and the Maccabean Jews. Both groups retreat to prepare for the next round of confrontation. The Hellenists, instead of humbly recognizing the divine omnipotence displayed through the miraculous Maccabee victory and seeking peace, arrogantly decide that the might of their hand will yet defeat God's purpose. They use the lull in the action to amass huge numbers of troops and to develop killing technology in an effort to ensure their victory over the Jews and Judaism.

The Jews, on the other hand, go on a "religious retreat," alighting to the traditional spiritual center established at Mitzpah Gilead. There they engage in a profound process of fasting, introspection, and repentance. Unlike the Hellenists, the Jews understand that their victory and survival ultimately depend not only on the human agency of military preparedness, but on divine providence.

Since God fights through divine agents, in this case the Maccabees, to save the world for religious freedom and morality, the battle ahead pits divine omnipotence against the earthy tyrannical power of the Syrian-Greeks.

As we read of the Maccabees' activities of rededication to the covenant in Mitzpah Gilead, we come to know more than just the lines of battle. The text teaches the value of spiritual preparation and the importance of periods of rejuvenation in our religious lives. It comes as no surprise that the very word "Chanukah" connotes rededication.

4:1	Then the evil Bagris boarded a ship	אָז נִכְנַס בַּגְרִיס הָרָשָׁע בִּסְפִינָה
4:2	and fled to king Antiochus, and with	וַיָּנָס אֶל אַנְטְיוֹכוֹס הַמֶּלֶךְ, וְעִמּוֹ
4:3	him were men who had escaped the sword.	אֲנָשִׁים פְּלִיטֵי חָרֶב.
4:4	Bagris spoke up and said to Antiochus,	וַיַּעַן בַּגְרִיס וַיֹּאמֶר לְאַנְטִיוֹכוֹס

4:5	the king, "You, the king,	הַמֶּלֶךְ: "אַתָּה, הַמֶּלֶךְ,
4:6	issued a command to abolish from	שַׂמְתָּ צַו לְבַטֵּל
4:7	the Jews the Sabbath, the festival of the	מִן הַיְּהוּדִים שַׁבָּת,
4:8	New Moon, and circumcision. And	רֹאשׁ חֹדֶשׁ וּמִילָה,
4:9	now there is a great rebellion in its	וְהִנֵּה מֶרֶד גָּדוֹל
4:10	midst, such that if all the peoples and	בְּתוֹכָהּ, אֲשֶׁר אִם [לֹא] יֵלְכוּ
4:11	nations and languages	כָּל הָעַמִּים וְהָאֻמּוֹת וְהַלְּשׁוֹנוֹת
	are not able to	לֹא יוּכְלוּ
4:12	attack, the five sons of Mattathias	לַחֲמֵשֶׁת בְּנֵי מַתִּתְיָה,
4:13	cannot be defeated; they are stronger than lions,	מֵאֲרָיוֹת הֵם חֲזָקִים,
4:14	swifter than eagles, and	וּמִנְּשָׁרִים הֵם קַלִּים
4:15	more rash than bears.	וּמִדֻּבִּים הֵם נִמְהָרִים.

P'shat: 4:1. the evil Bagris. Bagris's evil is further attested to by the upcoming episode. **4:2–3. and with him were men who had escaped the sword.** Instead of recognizing their defeat at the hands of the few as a sign of divine displeasure with their campaign against the Jews, and their survival as a chance to repent and live new and more righteous lives, Bagris and his men flee to Antiochus, bent on more evil. **4:8–9. And now there is a great rebellion.** The fact that Bagris is able to speak up to Antiochus and pin the great rebellion on the king's policies shows the confidence and power of Bagris. It also informs us, again, of Bagris's ethical culpability. He is no mere shill for the king. **4:10–11. all the peoples and nations and languages.** This phrase represents a combined force of all the varied subjects of the kingdom and again illustrates the isolation and long odds the Jewish people face in order to survive. **4:13–15. they are stronger than lions, swifter than eagles, and more rash than bears.** Although Bagris's statement confers praise upon the courage and military prowess of the Maccabees, he does not attribute their surprising success to any power beyond themselves. He still believes that the key to defeating the Maccabees, and hence the Jewish people, lies in his being able to assemble a large enough military force. **4:15. more rash than bears.** The Hebrew נִמְהַר (*nimaheir*) implies impetuousness and uncontrollability. Bears are known for formidable strength, as well as their ungovernable wrath when protecting their young.

D'rash: **4:1–2. boarded a ship and fled.** This echoes Jonah, who despite God's calling him to a prophetic mission, boards a ship in an effort to "flee to Tarshish from before the Eternal's presence (Jonah 1:3). Just as Jonah discovers the impossibility of escaping God's influence and power, so too will Bagris. **4:13. they are stronger than lions.** Jewish tradition uses the lion as a symbol of strength, courage, and majesty. Jacob, in his final blessing, compares Judah to a lion: "You, Judah: your brothers shall heap praise on you—your hand on the neck of your foes, your father's sons shall bow down to you. Judah is a lion's cub: you flourish, my son, from the prey. He kneels, crouches like a lion, like a lioness—who dare stir him up?" (Genesis 49:8–9). In fact, the lion has become the emblem of Judah, often depicted as protecting the Tablets of the Covenant. Proverbs 30:30 reminds us of the lion's hierarchal place: "The lion, the mightiest [or most heroic or brave] among beasts, he does not turn away for anyone."

4:14. swifter than eagles. This echoes the saying of Rabbi Y'hudah ben Teima: "Be as strong as a leopard, as swift [or light] as an eagle, as fast as a deer, and as brave as a lion to do the will of your Parent in heaven" (*Pirkei Avot* 5:20). Sixteenth-century Italian commentator Sforno notes that the lightness of the eagle implies the attainment of spiritual and ethical elevation. Eagles also connote freedom and rescue. Exodus 19:4 depicts God instructing Moses to remind the people, "You have seen what I did to the Egyptians, how I bore you on eagles' wings and brought you to Me." So too, do the actions of the Maccabees represent divine deliverance.

4:16 Now, O King,	עַתָּה הַמֶּלֶךְ,
4:17 be pleased to accept my advice,	עֲצָתִי תִּיטַב עָלֶיךָ,
if you attack them	אִם תִּלָּחֵם בָּהֶם
4:18 with this force, you will be	בְּחַיִל זֶה,
4:19 shamed in the eyes of all the	תֵּבוֹשׁ בְּעֵינֵי כָל
4:20 kings. Therefore, send letters to	הַמְּלָכִים. לָכֵן שְׁלַח סְפָרִים
4:21 all the provinces of your kingdom	בְּכָל מְדִינוֹת מַלְכוּתֶךָ,
4:22 and let military officers come; not	וְיָבוֹאוּ שָׂרֵי הַחֲיָלוֹת
4:23 one of them should remain; and	וְלֹא יִשָּׁאֵר מֵהֶם אֶחָד,
4:24 also elephants covered in	וְגַם פִּילִים מְלֻבָּשִׁים
4:25 armored plates should be	שִׁרְיוֹנִים יִהְיוּ
4:26 with them."	עִמָּהֶם".

P'shat: **4:17. accept my advice.** Again, Bagris cannot claim to only be following orders in attempting to destroy the Jewish people. Here, he seeks to initiate a new

57

round of battle, convincing the king of the next and proper course of action. **4:18. this force.** Bagris argues that the army the king has assembled is inadequate for the task at hand, subtly excusing his own failure in the recent defeat. **4:18–20. you will be shamed in the eyes of all the kings.** Understanding the nature and size of Antiochus's ego, Bagris need only appeal to the king's vanity to get what he wants. Bagris knows that Antiochus, like himself, is perfectly willing to spill human blood for the perceived enhancement of his glory. **4:22–23. not one of them should remain.** The fact that Bagris desires the assignment of every military officer in the empire illustrates his obsession with the destruction of the Jews. This goal obviously outweighs all other security concerns. **4:24–25. elephants covered in armored plates.** Such elephants might be considered the ancient Near Eastern equivalent of armored super-tanks. Certainly, they spelled a great technological and military advantage for the Syrian-Greeks, as the Jews did not possess anything like them.

D'rash: **4:20–21. Therefore, send letters to all the provinces of your kingdom.** This phrase echoes Esther 3:13, which depicts Haman sending letters to all the provinces of the kingdom informing them of their obligation to "exterminate all the Jews." But just as God, working in a hidden way through the actions of human beings, turned the tables on Haman, so too will divine providence working through the efforts of the Maccabees overturn Bagris's plan and punish him measure for measure. In contra-distinction to the letters of Bagris and Haman, II Maccabees depicts Y'hudah, the son of Mattathias, following the Jews' victory and rededication of the Temple, sending letters to all the Jewish communities that he had gathered holy scrolls to protect them from Antiochus's destructive wrath and would make these Scriptures available to all who would want to copy them. **4:22–23. not one of them should remain.** The struggle has reached a new phase. What began on Antiochus's part as a desire to destroy Judaism in order to convert the Jews to Hellenism has now devolved into an effort with complete annihilation as its goal. This of course illustrates the extreme results caused by a lack of religious tolerance, as well as the moral catastrophe of a world without the faithful practice of ethical monotheism as represented by Judaism. **4:24–25. elephants covered in armored plates.** Professors Henry Hyvernat and Emil G. Hirsch point out that elephants are not native to the ancient Near East. Their importation illustrates the "no expense spared" approach of the Syrian-Greeks to destroying the Jewish people.[1]

4:27	This thing was good in the eyes of	וַיִּיטַב הַדָּבָר בְּעֵינֵי
4:28	King Antiochus.	אַנְטִיוֹכוֹס הַמֶּלֶךְ,
	So he sent letters	וַיִּשְׁלַח סְפָרִים
4:29	to all the provinces of his kingdom, and	לְכָל מְדִינוֹת מַלְכוּתוֹ,
4:30	officers of the various peoples came,	וַיָּבוֹאוּ שָׂרֵי עַם וָעָם,
4:31	and with them were elephants covered	וְעִמָּהֶם פִּילִים מְלֻבָּשִׁים
4:32	in armored plates. The evil Bagris came	שִׁרְיוֹנִים. שֵׁנִית קָם בַּגְרִיס
4:33	to Jerusalem a second time. He split the	הָרָשָׁע וַיָּבוֹא לִירוּשָׁלָיִם, בָּקַע
4:34	wall, and broke the entranceway, and	הַחוֹמָה וַיְנַתֵּק הַמָּבוֹא
4:35	made thirteen breaches in the Temple,	וַיִּפְרֹץ בַּמִּקְדָּשׁ שְׁלֹשׁ עֶשְׂרֵה
4:36	and even smashed the stones until they	פְּרָצוֹת, וְגַם מִן הָאֲבָנִים שִׁבֵּר עַד
4:37	were as dust.	אֲשֶׁר הָיוּ כֶּעָפָר.
	He thought to himself,	וַיַּחְשֹׁב בְּלִבּוֹ וַיֹּאמַר:
4:38	"This time they will not defeat me,	"הַפַּעַם הַזֹּאת לֹא יוּכְלוּ לִי,
4:39	because my army is numerous and my	כִּי רַב חֵילִי
4:40	hand strong."	וְעַזָּה יָדִי".
4:41	But the God of the heavens did not	וֵאלֹהֵי הַשָּׁמַיִם לֹא
4:42	think thusly.	חָשַׁב כֵּן.

P'shat: **4:30. officers of the various peoples came.** According to I Maccabees 6:28–30, the king assembled his Friends, the official commanders of his army, and "masters of the horse" (literally, "those over the reins"), along with mercenaries from other kingdoms and even the Mediterranean islands. His army numbered one hundred thousand infantry, twenty thousand cavalry, and thirty-two trained war elephants. **4:31–32. elephants covered in armored plates.** I Maccabees 6:37 indicates that the Syrian-Greeks equipped each elephant with an armored and roofed wooden tower fastened by a special harness. They stationed two warriors to ride and fight from each tower. Each elephant also included an Indian driver. They distributed the elephants among the phalanxes (infantry formations); with each elephant they stationed a thousand men outfitted with coats of chain mail and brass helmets. A special force of five hundred handpicked horsemen was also assigned to each giant beast. **4:36–37. smashed the stones until they were as dust.** This again indicates the religious nature of this conflict, as well as the extreme animosity of the Syrian-Greeks toward Jewish religion.

D'rash: 4:35. thirteen breaches. *Mishnah Midot* 2:3 relates that the "idolatrous kings" made the thirteen breaches in the *soreig*, the latticework wall that surrounded the Temple court. The *soreig* marked the place beyond which non-Jews were not permitted to enter the courtyard proper. Its destruction, therefore, may point to the Syrian-Greek's misunderstanding concerning the "exclusive" nature of Judaism and "chosenness," misinterpreting issues of ritual purity as Jewish arrogance. Their misunderstanding apparently fed their anti-Jewish hatred. As for us, we understand that the concept of chosenness does not imply superiority, but obligation. Jews are not so much the Chosen People as we are the "choosing people." That is, anyone may choose to take on the obligations of the covenant, join the Jewish people, and pass into the holy "courtyard" of our faith. **4:39–40. my army is numerous and my hand strong.** Deuteronomy 8:14, 17 warns of the dangers of material prosperity: "Beware lest your heart grow haughty and you forget the Eternal your God—who freed you from the land of Egypt, the house of bondage . . . and you say to yourselves, 'My own power and the might of my own hand have won this wealth for me.'" **4:41–42. the God of the heavens did not think thusly.** This title indicates not only God's role as Creator, but continued divine rulership over all. An old Yiddish proverb states, "Man plans, but God laughs." Although Bagris intends to destroy the Temple, the Jews, and the covenant, and hence diminish God's influence in the world, the omnipotent King of kings, ruling through the efforts of God's agents, the Maccabees, will not allow this to happen.

4:43	When the five sons of Mattathias	כְּשָׁמֹעַ חֲמֵשֶׁת בְּנֵי מַתִּתְיָה,
4:44	heard, they got up and went to Mitzpeh	קָמוּ וַיָּבוֹאוּ לְמִצְפֵּה
4:45	Gilead, where the House of Israel had	גִלְעָד, אֲשֶׁר הָיְתָה שָׁם
4:46	been saved in the days of	פְּלֵיטָה לְבֵית יִשְׂרָאֵל בִּימֵי
4:47	Samuel, the prophet. They decreed a fast,	שְׁמוּאֵל הַנָּבִיא. צוֹם גָּזְרוּ,
4:48	and sat upon ashes, and sought	וַיֵּשְׁבוּ עַל הָאֵפֶר לְבַקֵּשׁ
4:49	mercy from before the God of the heavens.	רַחֲמִים מִלִּפְנֵי אֱלֹהֵי הַשָּׁמַיִם,
4:50	Then a good plan "fell into their heart."	אָז נָפְלָה בְּלִבָּם עֵצָה טוֹבָה.

P'shat: 4:44–45. Mitzpah Gilead. The name probably refers to a border outpost east of the Jordan River. Joshua 11:3 identifies Mitzpah as the place where the Israelites scored a great victory against several Canaanite kings. The medieval commentator Kimchi maintains that Joshua built an altar and a house of prayer and assembly in Mitzpah. **4:46–47. in the days of Samuel, the prophet.** Samuel called "all Israel" to

Mitzpah to purify themselves through *t'shuvah* (repentance), sacrifice, and prayer before successfully engaging the Philistines in battle (I Samuel 7:5–13). **4:47–48. They decreed a fast, and sat upon ashes.** Fasting and sitting in ashes imply *t'shuvah*, in that these actions are meant to induce a change in behavior. One must return to God in penitence, before seeking divine assistance. **4:48–49. sought mercy.** The Syrian-Greeks in their arrogance turn to weaponry. The Jews in humility reach up to God in humility. **4:50. Then a good plan "fell into their heart."** They were now ready to once again face the Syrian-Greeks in the battle that they obviously knew the enemy would press upon them.

D'rash: 4:44–45. Mitzpah Gilead. The name Mitzpah means "lookout" and, on one level, refers to the use of this outlying border outpost to protect against external attack. On another level, Mitzpah implies vigilance against the internal enemies of lack of faith, assimilation, and abandoning the covenant. As noted above, while the Syrian-Greeks prepare for the next confrontation by amassing a huge fighting force and armor-plated elephants, the Jews seek spiritual connection. **4:46–47. in the days of Samuel, the prophet.** Before gathering in Mitzpah, Samuel ordered the people, "Remove all foreign gods from your midst and the Ashtarot, and direct your heart to the Eternal and serve God alone, and God will save you from the hand of the Philistines" (I Samuel 7:3). Thus, the gathering at Mitzpah was associated not only with military victory, but with a rededication to Jewish religious identity and devotion to the Eternal. **4:46–47. in the days of Samuel, the prophet.** I Samuel 7:10 reports that God helped the Israelites in battle by thundering forth with a loud noise that threw the Philistines into a panic. **4:47. they decreed a fast.** *Mishnah Taanit* 2:3 states that public fasts should be proclaimed by the blast of the shofar. Jewish tradition associates the shofar, or ram's horn, with repentance (see Gleanings). **4:47–48. They decreed a fast, and sat upon ashes.** This parallels the three days of fasting that Queen Esther decrees when she learns of Haman's plot to murder all the Jews (Esther 4:16). The hope there and here is that the sincere repentance that emerges from the fast will move God to act in mercy on behalf of God's people. This also echoes Jonah 3:5–10, which depicts the Ninevites heeding the prophet's call to repentance. As part of this *t'shuvah* process, the Ninevites decree a fast, don sackcloth, and sit on ashes. **4:47–48. They decreed a fast, and sat upon ashes.** I Maccabees adds that they also rent their garments, opened a scroll of the Torah upon which Antiochus's men had drawn idols,[2] took the priestly vestments and the first fruits and the tithes, and assembled the Nazirites who had completed the periods of their vows.[3] They cried aloud to heaven, "What are we to do with these? Where are we to bring them? Your sanctuary has been trampled and profaned, and Your priests are in mourning and affliction. The gentiles have gathered against us to destroy us. You know what they are plotting against us. How shall we be able to withstand them, unless You come to our aid?'' (I Maccabees 3:50–53). **4:47–48. They decreed a fast, and sat upon ashes.** The disparity in approach between the Syrian-Greeks and the Jews echoes Psalm 20:8, ''Some rely upon chariots and some rely upon cavalry, but we call out in the name of the Eternal our God.'' **4:50. Then a good plan "fell into their heart."** One may assume that the plan ''fell'' from heaven as a result of their religious efforts. The use of the singular (''heart,'' as opposed to ''hearts'') speaks of the unity of the Maccabee forces at Mitzpah Gilead and parallels the unity of the Jewish people when they stood together at Mount Sinai to receive God's revelation: ''Israel encamped [וַיִּחַן, *vayichan*, conjugated in the singular] there in front of the mountain'' (Exodus 19:2). At Sinai the Jews received revelation and established the covenant that defined them as a people and gave them a spiritual reason to be. Their loyalty to the Sinaitic covenant proved to be the secret of Jewish survival and continuity. The Maccabees gathering at Mitzpah Gilead may be thought to represent a rededication to the covenant, its values and goals. The plan that falls into their heart may be regarded as a form of divine revelation. The Maccabees' example at Mitzpah Gilead also shines as a lesson for us. When we rededicate ourselves to the covenant, its values and goals and behaviors, our efforts can effect divine response. When we reach up to God in sincere *t'shuvah*, we can move God to mercy.

Fasting in Jewish Tradition

Following Bagris's initial defeat, he flees to Antiochus, who is located far from the field of battle. There, he prepares to attack the Jews yet again. He raises a huge army, larger than the previous one, equips them with weapons and armor, and even imports military technology. Bagris then returns to attack Jerusalem. He splits the wall, destroys the entranceway, and makes thirteen breaches in the Temple. He makes a point of pulverizing some of the Temple's stones.

The Jews, on the other hand, in preparation for the inevitable confrontation with Bagris and his army, go to the religious center at Mitzpah Gilead. There they fast, sit upon ashes, and pray. At first glance this behavior may seem strange, especially when faced with imminent danger, but a closer examination of the role of fasting in Jewish tradition may help make the Maccabees' behavior more understandable.

Jewish tradition sanctions spontaneous fasting, that is, a publicly promulgated fast made in response to some specific and exigent circumstance. The Maccabees' fast at Mitzpah Gilead is a case in point. The tradition also provides for public fast days that are fixed dates by the Hebrew calendar to be observed annually. Among these, the most well-known and widely observed is the fast sanctioned by the Torah, Yom Kippur, the Day of Atonement. We learn of the commandment in Leviticus 23:27: "Mark, the tenth day of this seventh month is the Day of Atonement. It shall be a sacred occasion for you: you shall practice self-denial." The Rabbis interpret "self-denial" to indicate five forbidden activities; the first among them is eating and/or drinking. As the name of this holy day implies, the abstention from food and drink is tied to the task at hand, namely achieving atonement. Relieved from concern for bodily nourishment, we may concentrate entirely on the needs of the soul. Also, keeping the fast demonstrates our good intentions to God, and the discomfort of the self-denial helps motivate us to make those changes necessary to effect a "coming home" to God, a turning to what is good and right, a return to a higher image of ourselves and who we may yet become.

The prophet Zechariah speaks of four other fixed public fasts: "the fast of the fourth month, and the fast of the fifth, and the fast of the seventh, and the fast of the tenth" (Zechariah 8:18). These four days commemorate our grief after the destruction of the Sanctuary, the holy city of Jerusalem, and the exile of our people from the Land.

The "fast of the fourth month" is (technically, in Zechariah's day) that of the ninth of Tammuz, the fourth month of the year according to the Bible's reckoning, as the Bible begins its count with Nisan. The Babylonians breached the walls of Jerusalem on the ninth of Tammuz in 586 B.C.E., an act that led to their destruction of the First Temple a month later on the ninth of Av. The Romans, however, on their way to destroying the Second Temple in the year 70 C.E., breached Jerusalem's walls on the seventeenth of Tammuz. The Rabbis chose the seventeenth to commemorate both breachings.

Tishah B'Av, or the Ninth of Av, is Zechariah's "fast of the fifth," as Av is the fifth month of the year (beginning as the Torah does with Nisan). This day commemorates the destruction of both Temples. Tishah B'Av and Yom Kippur are the only two sundown to sundown fasts of the calendar; all others begin with sunrise and end at sundown.

"The fast of the seventh" is known as Tzom G'daliah, or the Fast of Gedaliah. Jews fast on the third of Tishrei to mourn the assassination of Gedaliah, the son of Achikam, whom the Babylonians appointed governor after the destruction of the First Temple. The slaying moved the Babylonians to crush all hopes for Jewish autonomy in the Land of Israel and perpetrate a massive exile.

The Tenth of Tevet, "the fast of the tenth," marks the beginning of the Babylonian siege over Jerusalem, in 589 B.C.E., an act that caused much suffering and led directly to the Sanctuary's destruction three years hence.

In addition to the four fasts associated with the historical events surrounding the Temples' destructions and the exiles of our people, the Sages established two others: Taanit Esther, or the Fast of Esther, and the Fast of the Firstborn. The Fast of Esther occurs the day before Purim and commemorates the three days the Persian Jews fasted in response to Haman's edict of extermination and in anticipation of Esther's planned intercession with the king on behalf of her people. The Fast of the Firstborn occurs the day before Pesach. Firstborn sons customarily fast to commemorate how God saved "them" while at the same time slaying the firstborn of Egypt.

In addition to the set fasts of the Jewish year, *Mishnah Taanit* (2:3) teaches that in instances of impending doom, such as drought, earthquake, and/or war, the public authorities may proclaim a fast, such as those decreed by Esther and Mordechai in the case of Purim, the fast led by the Ninevite king as depicted in the Book of Jonah, or that declared by the Maccabees in our midrash.

What do all of these fasts have in common? Like the "great white fast" of Yom Kippur, all of these set fasts not only encourage Jewish solidarity, but urge us to purify ourselves in repentance. The Rabbis base this call to *t'shuvah* on the theological assumption that God transcends nature and vigilantly rules over everything. God challenges us, and God can save us. Therefore, any impending doom may be understood as a call to examine our behaviors in an effort to understand what we may have done to contribute to the situation and to understand just what God seeks to teach us through it. For instance, we read in *Pirkei Avot* 5:8–9 that drought and famine occur because of a failure to tithe in accordance with the commandments of the Torah, pestilence may result from transgressions involving the produce of the Sabbatical year, "the sword comes into the world because of justice delayed and justice denied and because of those who misinterpret the Torah" (5:8), false swearing and profaning God's name can result in an attack of wild animals, "exile comes to the world because of idolatry, sexual impropriety, bloodshed, and neglect of the Sabbatical release of the land" (5:9), and stealing from the poor will cause pestilence to increase. The Talmud teaches that the destruction of the Second Temple occurred because of "causeless hatred" (Babylonian Talmud, *Yoma* 9b).

Thus, the threat of annihilation posed by Bagris's attack upon the Temple and the Jewish people constitutes an opportunity for self-improvement on a personal and a national scale. In order to seek divine salvation and *chesed* (חֶסֶד), or covenantal kindness, the Maccabees and their followers must first show loyalty to the covenant themselves.

They must take an accounting of their souls, figure out where they have missed the mark, confess, promise to do better, and finally change their behaviors. Fasting not only demonstrates the people's sincerity before their divine partner, but motivates the people to do *t'shuvah*, to come closer to God in sincere repentance. Significantly, the Mishnah teaches us that public fasts would be proclaimed by the blast of the shofar, a symbol of repentance.

GLEANINGS

4:20–23 "send letters to all the provinces of your kingdom and let military officers come; not one of them should remain"

What Is Real?

War-making is one of the few activities that people are not supposed to view "realistically"; that is, with an eye to expense and practical outcome. In all-out war, expenditure is all-out, unprudent—war being defined as an emergency in which no sacrifice is excessive.

Susan Sontag, Illness as Metaphor
and AIDS and Its Metaphors
(New York: Picador, 2001), p. 99

4:47 "they decreed a fast"

The Shofar's Blast

[The shofar's blast] has a deep meaning, as if saying: "Awake, you sleeper, from your sleep! Rouse yourselves, you slumberers, out of your slumber! Examine your deeds, and turn to God in repentance. Remember your Creator, you who are caught up in the daily round, losing sight of eternal truth; you who are wasting your years in vain pursuits that neither profit nor save. Look closely at yourselves; improve your ways and your deeds. Abandon your evil ways, your unworthy schemes, every one of you![4]

Maimonides, Mishneh Torah, Hilchot T'shuvah 3:4

The Fast I Choose

Can this be the fast I choose, a day when a person merely afflicts himself? Can it be bowing his head like a bulrush and making a mattress of sackcloth and ashes? Do you call this a fast and a day of favor to the Eternal? Surely this is the fast I choose: open the bonds of wickedness, dissolve the groups that pervert justice, let the oppressed go free and annul all perverted justice...do not ignore your kin. Then your light will burst forth like the dawn and your healing will speedily sprout.

Isaiah 58:5–8

Chapter 5

Continuity versus Assimilation: These Were the Names...

One of the major overarching themes of *M'gillat Antiochus* is that of the Maccabean struggle against the assimilation to Greek ways that threatened Jewish survival. The military confrontation between Antiochus's forces and those of the Maccabees may be viewed as one aspect of a larger culture clash. This wider battle not only manifested in the Maccabees' opposition to the Syrian-Greeks, but in the pitting of all observant Jewry against those Jews who chose to adopt Hellenistic ways.

The Hellenizing Jews abandoned the Sinaitic covenant of their ancestors to adopt Greek ways, mores, and religious practices. The taking of Greek names like Menelaus, Lysimachus, and Jason proved to be a prominent symbol of their assimilation.

Jews loyal to the covenant continued to call themselves by traditional Hebrew and especially biblical names. These names illustrated their steadfast commitment to Jewish identity and their devotion to Judaism. Not surprisingly, all of the Hasmonean brothers bore Hebrew names.

5:1	And these were their names:	וְהָיוּ שְׁמוֹתֵיהֶם
5:2	Y'hudah, the firstborn;	יְהוּדָה הַבְּכוֹר,
	Shimon, the second;	שִׁמְעוֹן הַשֵּׁנִי,
5:3	Yochanan, the third; Yonatan, the fourth;	יוֹחָנָן הַשְּׁלִישִׁי, יוֹנָתָן הָרְבִיעִי,
5:4	Elazar, the fifth.	אֶלְעָזָר הַחֲמִישִׁי.
	Their father blessed them	וַיְבָרֶךְ אוֹתָם אֲבִיהֶם
5:5	before he sent them to the war;	קֹדֶם שֶׁשְּׁלָחָם לַמִּלְחָמָה,
	he said to	וַיֹּאמֶר
5:6	them, "Y'hudah, my son,	לָהֶם: "יְהוּדָה בְּנִי,
	I compare you to	אֲדַמֶּה אוֹתְךָ

66

5:7	Y'hudah, son of Yaakov,	לִיהוּדָה בֶּן יַעֲקֹב
	who was likened	אֲשֶׁר הָיָה נִמְשָׁל
5:8	to a lion. Shimon, my son,	לְאַרְיֵה. שִׁמְעוֹן בְּנִי,
	I compare you	אֲדַמֶּה אוֹתְךָ
5:9	to Shimon, son of Yaakov, who killed the	לְשִׁמְעוֹן בֶּן יַעֲקֹב אֲשֶׁר הָרַג
5:10	inhabitants of Sh'chem.	יוֹשְׁבֵי שְׁכֶם.
5:11	Yochanan, my son, I compare you to	יוֹחָנָן בְּנִי, אֲדַמֶּה אוֹתְךָ
5:12	Avner, son of Ner, general of Israel's army.	לְאַבְנֵר בֶּן נֵר, שַׂר צְבָא יִשְׂרָאֵל.
5:13	Yonatan, my son,	יוֹנָתָן בְּנִי,
5:14	I compare you to Yonatan, son of Shaul,	אֲדַמֶּה אוֹתְךָ לְיוֹנָתָן בֶּן שָׁאוּל
5:15	who killed the Philistine people.	אֲשֶׁר הָרַג עִם פְּלִשְׁתִּים.
5:16	Elazar, my son,	אֶלְעָזָר בְּנִי,
	I compare you to Pinchas	אֲדַמֶּה אוֹתְךָ לְפִינְחָס
5:17	son of Elazar, who was zealous	בֶּן אֶלְעָזָר, אֲשֶׁר קִנֵּא
5:18	for his God and saved	לֵאלֹהָיו וְהִצִּיל
5:19	the Children of Israel."	אֶת בְּנֵי יִשְׂרָאֵל."

***P'shat*: 5:1. And these were their names.** All of the brothers have Hebrew names steeped in Jewish history (each comes from the Bible), as opposed to the Greek names sported by the assimilationists. **5:4. Their father blessed them.** Mattathias girds them for battle by offering them role models of Jewish military prowess and zealotry for God's purpose. The blessing, of course, is a prayer that they manifest the best qualities of their namesakes. **5:4. Their father blessed them.** Mattathias's blessing of his sons at this point may be regarded as more than a charge to battle. A father blessing his children shortly before his death is a well-attested ancient custom. Mattathias's blessing here may indicate that he has become ever increasingly aware of his mortality.

***D'rash*: 5:1. And these were their names.** This echoes the beginning of the Book of Exodus, "And these are the names of the Children of Israel." This second book of the Torah, of course, presents the tale of the slavery, redemption, birth of the Jewish people as a nation, and the establishment of the covenant at Sinai. **5:1. names.** The midrash *Shir HaShirim Rabbah* 4:25 teaches that one reason our people deserved to be redeemed from Egyptian slavery was that they kept their Hebrew names:

"As Reuven and Shimon they went down to Egypt, and as Reuven and Shimon they went up from it. They did not call Reuven Rufus, nor did they call Shimon Luliani."
5:4. Their father blessed them. This echoes Jacob gathering and blessing his sons before his death and charging them with the sacred task of carrying the torch of God's light into the future, as depicted in Genesis 49:1–28. This section also parallels I Maccabees 2:49–70, which presents Mattathias gathering his sons before him for a blessing shortly before his death. He calls for his sons to "be zealous for the Torah," to display the "faith under trial" of Abraham, the mitzvah observance of Joseph (who observed despite personal distress), the zeal of Pinchas, the strength and leadership of Joshua, the courage of Caleb (who stood up against the evil report of the spies before the congregation), the piety of David, the zeal on behalf of the Torah shown by Elijah, the devotion of Hananiah, Azariah, and Mishael (who had the faith to march into the fiery furnace for God), and the guiltless nature of Daniel (whom God saved from lions). **5:6. I compare you (אֲדַמֶּה אוֹתְךָ).** The 1725 manuscript of Rafael Chaim me-Italya reads אוֹדֶה מִמְּךָ, "I will give thanks because of you." Thus, Mattathias, in addition to expressing filial love, offers a foreshadowing of the debt of gratitude that he and all Jews will owe Y'hudah and his brother Maccabees for their heroic efforts in saving Judaism and the Jewish people. **5:7–8. Y'hudah, son of Yaakov, who was likened to a lion.** Jacob (Yaakov) declares of his son Y'hudah (Judah), "You, Judah, your brothers shall heap praise on you—your hand on the neck of your foes . . . like a lioness—who dare stir him up?" (Genesis 49:8–9). I Maccabees 3:4 also compares Y'hudah to a lion: "He was like a lion in his deeds, like a lion's cub roaring for prey."
5:9–10. Shimon son of Yaakov, who killed the inhabitants of Sh'chem. Genesis 34 relates the story of Jacob's sons Levi and Shimon (Simon) slaughtering the inhabitants of Sh'chem in defending the honor of their sister, Dinah, who was raped at the hands of the local prince (also known as Sh'chem). Although many commentators debate the justice of the brother's rampage, the apocryphal Book of Judith praises Shimon's zeal by thanking God for providing Shimon's sword "to take revenge on those strangers who had torn off a virgin's clothing to defile her, and exposed her thighs to put her to shame, and polluted her womb to disgrace her; for you said, 'It shall not be done'" (Judith 9:2). According to scholar Judith A. Kates, the rape motif evidenced in the above verse not only refers to Sh'chem's crime against Dinah, but also Holofernes's invasion of the Land of Israel. Desecrating the Temple, then, may be considered tantamount to forcibly polluting the spiritual "womb" of the Jewish people, disseminating ritual and ethical impurity from the Jews' sacred life-giving, inner core, and causing the people's religious future to be barren. The fact that the "town of hill passes, chosen to defend the narrow, tightly closed access to that vulnerable inner

space is called Bethulia, which resonates with the Hebrew *'betulah'*—virgin,'' further emphasizes Kates's point.[1] **5:11. Yochanan.** The Bible does mention two men named Yochanan. I Chronicles 3:15 cites King Josiah's firstborn as Yochanan. According to the Talmud (*Horayot* 11b), he was also known as Jehoahaz and was the first of Josiah's sons to occupy the throne of Judah. He reigned for only three months before being captured by Pharaoh Neco and hence was removed from power (II Kings 23:33–34). The other biblical Yochanan, Yochanan son of Kareah, was an officer under Gedaliah son of Ahikam, whom the Babylonians appointed as governor over Judah following the destruction of the First Temple in 586 B.C.E. Yochanan urged the populace to submit to Babylonian hegemony and warned Gedaliah that an assassin sought his life. Gedaliah did not heed Yochanan's advice for caution. He was killed in 582 B.C.E. Exile and many hardships then fell upon the Jewish people (Jeremiah 40:7–16). It may be assumed that due to the inglorious nature of the careers of these two biblical Yochanans, Mattathias chose instead to mention Avner son of Ner in connection with his son. **5:12. Avner son of Ner.** Avner was the uncle of King Shaul (Saul) and the commander of his army. Avner eventually recognized David as God's anointed and helped consolidate the kingdom under David's control. *Kohelet Rabbah* 9:11 recounts his great physical prowess: ''It was easier for a person to move a wall six cubits thick than to move one of Avner's feet.'' The Talmud speaks of his righteousness in refusing to obey Saul's order to murder the priests of Nob (Babylonian Talmud, *Sanhedrin* 49a). **5:14. Yonatan, son of Shaul.** Yonatan (Jonathan) was Saul's eldest son, who recognized the divine choice of David to succeed his father. He befriended David and helped him escape Saul's insane wrath. Jonathan's bravery in the wars against the Philistines won him great respect among the people. **5:16–17. Pinchas son of Elazar.** Numbers 25 depicts God offering Pinchas the ''covenant of peace'' and eternal priesthood for his act of zealotry, in slaughtering a royal couple who publically fornicated at the entrance of the Tent of Meeting. This turned back a plague that had threatened the existence of the Jewish people during the forty years of wandering in the wilderness.

5:20 After this, the five sons of Mattathias	אַחַר זֶה קָמוּ חֲמֵשֶׁת בְּנֵי מַתִּתְיָה
5:21 rose up and fought against those	וַיִּלָּחֲמוּ בָּעַמִּים הָהֵם,
5:22 peoples, and they wrought a great	וַיַּהַרְגוּ בָהֶם
5:23 slaughter against them. But, of them,	הֶרֶג רַב,
5:24 Y'hudah was killed.	וַיֵּהָרֵג מֵהֶם יְהוּדָה.
5:25 Immediately, when the children of	בְּאוֹתָה שָׁעָה, כַּאֲשֶׁר רָאוּ בְּנֵי

5:26	Mattathias saw that Y'hudah had been killed,	מַתִּתְיָה כִּי נֶהֱרַג יְהוּדָה,
5:27	they turned back and came to	שָׁבוּ וַיָּבוֹאוּ אֶל
5:28	their father, and he said to them,	אֲבִיהֶם, וַיֹּאמֶר לָהֶם:
5:29	"Why have you returned?"	"לָמָה שַׁבְתֶּם".
5:30	They spoke up and said,	וַיַּעֲנוּ וַיֹּאמְרוּ:
5:31	"Because Y'hudah, our brother, who alone	"עַל אֲשֶׁר נֶהֱרַג יְהוּדָה אָחִינוּ,
5:32	equaled all of us, has been killed."	אֲשֶׁר הָיָה חָשׁוּב כְּכֻלָּנוּ".
5:33	Mattathias answered,	וַיַּעַן מַתִּתְיָה וַיֹּאמֶר אֲלֵיהֶם:
	"I will go out	"אֲנִי אֵצֵא
5:34	with you and fight against the peoples,	עִמָּכֶם וְאֶלָּחֵם
5:35	lest they destroy the House	בָּעַמִּים, פֶּן יְאַבְּדוּ בֵּית
5:36	of Israel, and you remain dismayed over	יִשְׂרָאֵל, וְאַתֶּם נִבְהַלְתֶּם עַל
5:37	your brother."	אֲחִיכֶם".

P'shat: 5:20. After this. That is, following Mattathias's blessing and charge. **5:21. rose up and fought.** The Maccabees "rise to the occasion" and fight valiantly despite being greatly outnumbered and lacking the technology that the enemy had brought to the battlefield. **5:21–22. those peoples.** Another reminder of the great odds that the brothers and their Jewish followers faced as they fought against the huge army of many nationalities that Antiochus had gathered upon Bagris's advice. **5:23. of them.** Of the five brothers, Y'hudah, the firstborn, their leader, perishes in the battle. **5:27. they turned back.** Shimon, Yonatan, Yochanan, and Elazar leave the battlefield to mourn for their fallen brother, Y'hudah. **5:33–34. I will go out with you.** Despite his advanced age, Mattathias heroically puts himself on the line in combat in order to save the Jewish people. This behavior represents a distinction from that of Antiochus, who orders others to do his bidding while personally remaining many miles away from any fighting and/or perceived danger. **5:35–36. lest they destroy the House of Israel.** Mattathias explains that the survival of the Jewish people at this critical time of crisis must take precedence over a formal period of mourning for their brother, and his son. **5:36–37. and you remain dismayed over your brother.** Mattathias apparently fears that the brothers will be immobilized by their mourning, unable to meet the challenges of Bagris's ensuing attacks.

D'rash: 5:24. Y'hudah was killed. According to both I Maccabees 9:4–21 and Josephus's *Antiquities* 12.11.2, Y'hudah died after the cleansing and rededication of the Temple, not before. Jonathan A. Goldstein, in his commentary to the Books of the Maccabees, calculates that Y'hudah and his brothers purified and rededicated the Temple on the twenty-fifth of Kislev, 164 B.C.E., and posits the year of Y'hudah's death to have been 160 B.C.E.[2] Clearly, *M'gillat Antiochus* makes religious truth its priority, as opposed to historical accuracy. **5:27–28. they turned back and came to their father.** Normative Jewish mourning practice calls for the immediate family of the deceased to "sit shivah" for the first week following the burial; that is, the family remains in their home for the first seven days following the burial and sits on stools low to the ground as an expression of grief. According to Rabbi Maurice Lamm, this bereavement ritual represents "a physical adjustment to one's emotional state, a lowering of the body to the level of one's feelings, a symbolic enactment of remorse and desolation."[3] **5:35. lest they destroy the House of Israel.** As is the case with the laws of Shabbat, the traditions of mourning may be overridden in order to save life.

5:38	So Mattathias went out that day with his	וַיֵּצֵא מַתִּתְיָה בַּיּוֹם הַהוּא עִם
5:39	sons, and they fought against the peoples.	בָּנָיו, וַיִּלָּחֲמוּ בָּעַמִּים.
5:40	The God of the heavens gave all the	וֵאלֹהֵי הַשָּׁמַיִם נָתַן כָּל
5:41	soldiers of the peoples into their hand, and	גִּבּוֹרֵי הָעַמִּים בְּיָדָם,
5:42	they effected a great slaughter.	וַיַּהַרְגוּ בָהֶם הֶרֶג רָב,
5:43	Of every swordsman and every archer,	כָּל שׁוֹלֵף חֶרֶב וְכָל אוֹחֵז קֶשֶׁת,
5:44	army officers and high officials,	שָׂרֵי הַחַיִל וְהַסְּגָנִים,
	not one of	לֹא נוֹתַר בָּהֶם
5:45	them survived, and the rest of the people	שָׂרִיד, וַיָּנוּסוּ שְׁאָר הָעַמִּים
5:46	fled to the coastal provinces.	לִמְדִינוֹת הַיָּם.
5:47	But Elazar was engaged in killing the	וְאֶלְעָזָר הָיָה מִתְעַסֵּק לְהָמִית
5:48	elephants when he became engulfed in	הַפִּילִים, וַיִּטְבַּע בְּפֶרֶשׁ הַפִּילִים,
5:49	elephant dung. His brothers searched for	וַיְבַקְשׁוּהוּ אֶחָיו בֵּין
5:50	him among the living and among the dead,	הַחַיִּים וּבֵין הַמֵּתִים וְלֹא
5:51	but they could not find him.	מְצָאוּהוּ,
5:52	Eventually, they found him	וְאַחֲרֵי כֵן מְצָאוּהוּ
5:53	buried in the elephant dung.	טוֹבֵעַ בְּפֶרֶשׁ הַפִּילִים.

P'shat: **5:38. So Mattathias went out that day.** A man of his word, Mattathias goes out that very day, leading his sons into battle. **5:38–39. with his sons, and they fought.** Despite their initial impulse to stay home and mourn, the brothers honor

71

their father by heeding his instructions to defend the House of Israel. **5:40. God of the heavens.** Once again, the midrash reminds us that the Maccabees' victory is due to divine power. The mention of divine assistance at this point also testifies to the soundness of their decision to fight for the Jewish people at this specific juncture, despite the mourning period for their brother, Y'hudah. **5:44–45. not one of them survived.** This obvious hyperbole indicates that the Maccabees routed the enemy. **5:47–48. engaged in killing the elephants.** The term "engaged" connotes the ongoing efforts of Elazar. Taking down the Syrian-Greek tanklike elephants proved to be neither simple nor quick. Elazar heroically took upon himself the most difficult, dangerous, and apparently dirtiest of tasks.

***D'rash*: 5:47–48. engaged in killing the elephants.** This echoes I Maccabees 6:43–46 which reports that Elazar noticed that one of the elephants bore royal armor and stood taller than the others. Assuming that the king rode atop, "boldly he dashed into the midst of the phalanx at the elephant, slaying men right and left as he cut the enemy down on both sides of his path. Going in underneath the elephant, he stabbed it to death, whereupon the elephant fell to the ground on top of him, killing him there." **5:52–53. they found him buried in the elephant dung.** In the words of I Maccabees 6:44, "Elazar gave his life to save his people and win eternal fame." Sometimes heroic and righteous measures require the humility involved in literally getting one's hands dirty.

The Importance of Names in Jewish Tradition: A Brief Examination of Biblical Names

Shakespeare wrote: "What's in a name? That which we call a rose, by any other name would smell as sweet."[4] By this statement Shakespeare demonstrated that he was neither Jewish nor a dedicated biblical scholar, because Jewish tradition, from its biblical roots through the present era, has consistently placed great emphasis upon names.

Names in Judaism bear many functions. Names spell identity. They speak of one's heritage, both familial and religious. Names represent status. Changes in names mark changes in one's stature. Names can provide meaning and mission in life.

This emphasis upon names begins with the very first Jews, Abraham and Sarah. The Torah, in Genesis 17:5, depicts God changing the name of the patriarch from Avram (אַבְרָם, "the father of a people") to Avraham (אַבְרָהָם, "the father of many peoples"). Similarly, in Genesis 17:15, Abraham's wife, at God's behest, goes from being Sarai

(שָׂרַי, "my princess") to become Sarah (שָׂרָה, "princess").[5] Both Abraham's and Sarah's names receive the Hebrew letter *hei* (ה), a letter "borrowed" from the ineffable four-letter name of the Eternal (י-ה-ו-ה), indicative of their spiritual transformation and their arrival to a higher plane of holiness. Having overcome various trials, Abraham and Sarah have grown to become "spiritual giants" achieving new levels of covenantal relationship with God. Their new names communicate their elevated status.

Of course, spiritual status does not necessarily only rise. Dimunition may also be communicated through names. For instance, we find that when Abraham purchases a burial plot for his beloved Sarah from Efron the Hittite, the latter charges the patriarch four-hundred shekels of silver "in negotiable currency." The Talmud (*Bava M'tzia* 87a) explains that each shekel Abraham paid was worth twenty-five hundred ordinary shekels, indicating the exorbitance of the price. Throughout chapter 23 of Genesis, which chronicles the transaction, the Torah spells Efron's name *malei*, or full (with the Hebrew letter *vav*, עֶפְרוֹן), but once the money changes hands, Scripture spells his name *chaseir* (without the *vav*, עֶפְרֹן). Thus, his "new name" implies that his moral stature has been diminished by his taking advantage of Abraham in his hour of need.

The Torah further emphasizes the importance of names not only by changing them, but by whom the text identifies by name and whom it does not. Exodus 1:15–21 depicts a contest between the king of Egypt and the Hebrew midwives. The king tells the Hebrew midwives to murder all Jewish male babies upon birth, but the midwives refuse to carry out such an evil decree, out of respect for God and God's laws of morality. Significantly, the Torah never mentions the king's name, referring to him with the generic "Pharaoh" or simply as "king of Egypt." On the other hand, the text reveals the midwives' names as Shiphrah (שִׁפְרָה), meaning "beauty" (Rashi comments that she beautified the babies when they were born), and Puah (פּוּעָה), which means "crying out, cooing" (for she cried out and cooed in order to calm the babies). These names indicate something of the essence of these women, indicating that they not only possessed physical beauty, but exhibited an inner moral splendor by their acts of righteousness calmly performed under severe pressure. Scripture explains that they stood in "awe of God," and God rewarded them with "houses." Rashi specifies that the houses in question were not buildings; rather, God blessed the midwives with continuity, as they became progenitors of royalty.

Names in Jewish tradition reflect values, theology, and the historical roots of the family or person bearing it. For instance, Isaac's name, Yitzchak, means "he will laugh." He-Will-Laugh may seem a strange or inauspicious title for a future patriarch. According to scholar Naomi Rosenblatt, however, the name embraces the spiritual significance of his parents' reaction to news of his impending birth and marks the first time that laughter is mentioned in the Bible. The name captures Abraham and Sarah's incredulity and arrant giddiness at God's promise to bestow a child upon a ninety-year-old woman and a ninety-nine-year-old man. The news moves them to laughter. Isaac's name reminds Abraham and Sarah, and instructs us that "while human faith has limits, God's power to perform wondrous deeds is infinite."[6]

Names speak of one's heritage, both familial and religious. As mentioned above, *Shir HaShirim Rabbah* (4:25) teaches that one of the reasons the Children of Israel deserved to be redeemed from Egypt was the fact that they kept their Hebrew names, even in the direst straits. These names not only forged a link with their earliest ancestors, helping the people to connect with their roots, but also signaled Jewish pride and loyalty to the covenant.

But even more than that, each name acts as a charge to a mission, a glimpse into one's personal destiny. Although Exodus 2:10 depicts Pharaoh's daughter naming the baby she finds in the reeds of the Nile "Mosheh," explaining, "I drew him out of the water," his name is not parsed in the passive and does not mean "drawn from the water." Rather, the name Mosheh is couched in the active and is better translated "he draws out [rescues, extricates]." Hence, the name charges Moses with the destiny of becoming God's agent to rescue the Children of Israel from bondage. His mission will be to extricate the Jewish people from the straits of Egypt and to draw the people through the Reed Sea on their way to Mount Sinai.

Just as Moses is charged with a mission, so too are his namesakes. This is why *M'gillat Antiochus* presents Mattathias reviewing the names of his sons. The names not only honor those who came before, but present a challenge to the sons. Each name serves as a prayer that the one bearing it will live up to the legacies of those who preceded him—that they will proudly manifest the best traits of their ancestors, carry forward the life of the Jewish people, and bring healing to the world.

It is significant that each covenantal ceremony, the *b'rit milah* for boys and the *b'rit bat* or *shalom bat* for girls, also features an official Hebrew naming. And each ceremony includes a *kisei Eliyahu*, a chair of Elijah the prophet. This reminds us that in Jewish tradition Elijah is not only considered the protector of the poor, but the harbinger of the messianic era. Since no one knows the identity of the Messiah, we celebrate the potential of every child who comes into our midst to do great things. Every child may be the one to save the Jewish people and bring healing to the world. Each name expresses the hope that the one bearing it will live up to his or her personal destiny to bring humanity closer to perfection.

GLEANINGS

5:1 *"And these were their names"*

A Parent's Hope

Names reflect a person's character and destiny, and a parent's hope. In the Torah, both fathers and mothers bestow names—as does God. In names we find the roots of much Jewish history. In fact, much of the drama of Genesis revolves around the giving of names.

Ellen Frankel, The Five Books of Miriam, p. 20

A Good Name

Every time a person increases his performance of mitzvot, he earns a good name for himself. You find that a person is called by three names: one that his mother and father call him, one that other people call him, and one that he earns for himself. The one that he earns for himself is superior to all of them.

Tanchuma, Vayak'heil 1

5:1 *"And these were their names"*

Each of Us Has a Name

Each of us has a name
given by God
and given by our parents

Each of us has a name
given by our stature and our smile
and given by what we wear

Each of us has a name
given by the mountains
and given by our walls

Each of us has a name
given by the stars
and given by our neighbors

Each of us has a name
given by our sins
and given by our longings

Each of us has a name
given by our enemies
and given by our love

Each of us has a name
given by our celebrations
and given by our work

Each of us has a name
given by the seasons
and given by our blindness

Each of us has a name
given by the sea
and given by
our death.

Zelda, The Spectacular Difference:
Selected Poems of Zelda, trans. Marcia Falk
(New York: HUC Press, 2004), p. 141–143.

Authenticity

And then we began to write our own names as people to define ourselves, and to know the strength that authenticity gives you.

We didn't have that sense of authenticity from our Jewish experience if we grew up as I did in an assimilated, almost anti-Jewish community. There was the fixing of noses, the changing of names.

Betty Friedan, "Jewish Roots: An Interview
with Betty Friedan," Tikkun, Jan./Feb. 1988

Inside, Outside

Right now there is the matter of my name.

Not a complicated point, you might think; but you would be wrong.

To begin with, every Jew who has ever stepped into a synagogue or temple knows that we have two names: the outside name with which we go through life, and the inside name, the Jewish name, used in blessings and Torah call-ups, marriage and divorce ceremonies, and on tombstones. No shammas or sexton...has ever summoned me to the Torah as "Mr. I. David Goodkind." Unthinkable. I am "Reb Yisroel Dovid ben Eliyahu." We usually are named in Hebrew after relatives who have passed on;[7] then the parents try to find some outside name that will at least have the same first letter.

It is a far-drifted Jew who has forgotten his or her inside name.

Herman Wouk, *Inside, Outside*,[8] pp. 36–37

5:4 *"Their father blessed them"*

Unity

Jacob called his sons together so he could share with each of them what would happen to them in the days to come. Unlike his forbearers, he included all his sons in his final blessings. To be sure, each of his sons was different and each deserved a distinctive blessing, but none would be left out. All would have a share in the blessing that had been given originally to Abraham and transmitted through Isaac. They were one people, one nation, and through their unity they would not only survive but flourish. Unity was the most important condition for Israel's redemption.

Norman Cohen, *Voices From Genesis*, p. 146

Personal Identity

The most enduring legacy we can bequeath to our children is a clear articulation of who we are and what we stand for. We can leave them financial assets, but those can lose their value. A family business can go bankrupt. A family home can burn down. But if we can make clear to our children who we are, where we have come from, and what we value, then they can begin to build their own personal identity based on a solid foundation.

Naomi H. Rosenblatt and Joshua Horwitz, *Wrestling with Angels*, p. 376

5:38–39 *"So Mattathias went out that day with his sons, and they fought against the peoples."*

Discouraging Injustice

If I practice love to the extent that when you smite me on the right cheek, I offer you the left also, I am thereby encouraging injustice. I, like you, am then guilty of the injustice that is practiced.

Ahad Ha'am, quoted in Joseph Telushkin, *Jewish Wisdom*, p. 420

Chapter 6

Tradition versus Innovation:
The Establishment of Chanukah

The establishment of the postbiblical holiday of Chanukah represents not only the final chapter of *M'gillat Antiochus*, but a new chapter in Jewish history. Up to this point, the revelation born of prophecy found in the Torah determined the Festivals of the year. The Maccabees do not claim to be prophets or the deputies of prophets. Rather, they seek to establish the Chanukah celebration upon the strength of their authority as interpreters of Torah. The priests, Levites, and Sages then utilize their authority as teachers of Torah to confirm the postbiblical festival as one to be kept from generation to generation.

In the process, not only does the eight-day festival born of the Maccabees' miraculous victory become a permanent fixture of the Jewish calendar, but the turning point from a traditional world of revelation to a new epic of innovation based upon Torah knowledge and interpretation. This historical "rite of passage" becomes a cause for celebration.

6:1	The Children of Israel rejoiced, for	וַיִּשְׂמְחוּ בְּנֵי יִשְׂרָאֵל כִּי
6:2	their enemies had been given over into their hands.	נִתְּנוּ בִידֵיהֶם שׂוֹנְאֵיהֶם,
6:3	Some of them they burned	מֵהֶם שָׂרְפוּ
6:4	with fire, and some of them they hanged	בָּאֵשׁ, וּמֵהֶם תָּלוּ
6:5	upon a tree, and the Children of Israel	עַל הָעֵץ,
6:6	immolated the evil Bagris, the one	וּבַגְרִיס הָרָשָׁע, הַמַּטְעֶה אֶת עַמּוֹ,
6:7	who caused his people to err. And when	שָׂרְפוּ אוֹתוֹ בְּנֵי יִשְׂרָאֵל בָּאֵשׁ.
6:8	Antiochus the king	וְאַנְטִיּוֹכוֹס הַמֶּלֶךְ
	heard that they had	כַּאֲשֶׁר שָׁמַע אֲשֶׁר
6:9	killed his governor Bagris and all the	נֶהֶרְגוּ בַגְרִיס מִשְׁנֵהוּ וְכָל

77

6:10	army officers with him,	שָׂרֵי הַחַיִל אֲשֶׁר עִמּוֹ,
	he boarded a ship	נִכְנַס בִּסְפִינָה
6:11	and fled to the coastal provinces.	וַיָּנָס לִמְדִינוֹת הַיָּם.
6:12	And it happened that every place he	וַיְהִי כָּל מָקוֹם אֲשֶׁר הָיָה
6:13	would go, they would rebel against him	בָא שָׁמָּה הָיוּ מוֹרְדִים בּוֹ
6:14	and call him, "the Fugitive," so he	וְקוֹרְאִים אוֹתוֹ הַבּוֹרֵחַ,
6:15	threw himself into the sea.	וַיַּשְׁלֵךְ אֶת נַפְשׁוֹ הַיָּמָּה.

P'shat: **6:1. The Children of Israel rejoiced.** The Jews rejoice in the divine salvation that has been wrought for them. **6:3–5. Some of them they burned with fire, and some of them they hanged upon a tree.** The Mishnah (*Sanhedrin* 7:1) prescribes burning and hanging (strangling) as punishments legally meted out to capital criminals by a court of law: burning for certain cases of sexual immorality, especially incest (see Leviticus 20:14 and *Mishnah Sanhedrin* 9:1); and strangling for adultery, one who strikes his father or his mother, one who kidnaps an individual in order to sell him or her into slavery, and a false prophet who prophesies in the name of an idol (see Rashi to Leviticus 20:10, Exodus 21:15, Deuteronomy 24:7, Deuteronomy 18:20, and *Mishnah Sanhedrin* 11:1). Alternately, hanging and burning may also refer to public displays made subsequent to death (Deuteronomy 21:22–23; II Kings 23:20).[1] The authorities utilized such methods so as to illustrate justice at work, stigmatize the practice of evil in the eyes of the people, and thereby deter crime. **6:10–11. boarded a ship and fled.** Like many a bully, Antiochus runs in defeat. His flight serves as testimony to his arrant cowardice. His behavior stands in contrast to the bravery and heroism of the Maccabees. **6:10–11. he boarded a ship and fled.** Antiochus's actions, like those of Bagris before him (see 4:1–2), echo Jonah's "going down" and boarding a ship in attempting to flee from God's presence (Jonah 1:3). Just as Jonah cannot go anyplace where God is not, so too will Antiochus experience the impossibility of fleeing the Divine Presence. **6:11. fled to the coastal provinces.** These were Greek strongholds where Antiochus would have thought himself safe. **6:13–14. they would rebel against him and call him "the Fugitive."** The empire's once subdued subjects no longer fear Antiochus, nor do they show him any respect. The king, who at the beginning of the midrash declared himself Epiphanes, or "god manifest," and terrorized others and burned down their temples with seeming impunity, is now on the run. His new title, "the Fugitive," signals this change in status. **6:14–15. he threw himself into the sea.** Antiochus commits suicide. According to the laws of Judaism, suicide is tantamount to the sin of murder and hence a sign of ignominious dishonor.

***D'rash*: 6:1. The Children of Israel rejoiced.** This parallels Esther 8:16, which reports that after the tables are turned upon the evil Haman and his henchmen, "the Jews had light and gladness, and joy and honor." It must be mentioned that although the Children of Israel rejoice in gratitude at their deliverance from annihilation, Jewish law forbids taking pleasure from someone else's suffering, even an enemy. Thus we read in Proverbs 24:17, "If your enemy falls, do not celebrate. If he trips, let not your heart rejoice." Rabbi Yochanan again illustrates this point in the Talmud (*M'gillah* 10b): "The Holy One does not rejoice at the downfall of the wicked.... The ministering angels tried to recite a song of praise to God when the Egyptians were drowning in the Reed Sea. However, the Holy One exclaimed, 'My handiwork is drowning in the sea and you recite a song?'" **6:3. Some of them they burned.** *Mishnah Sanhedrin* 9:1 legislates burning as the punishment for one who has sexual intercourse with a woman and her daughter (see Leviticus 18:17) and expands this law to include other cases of incest. Hence, the mention of burning here hints at the profligate nature of Hellenistic culture and its proponents and practitioners. II Kings 23:20 depicts King Josiah, as part of his spiritually purifying reformation, burning the bones of Jeroboam, the profligate Israelite king who promoted idolatry by building temples in Beth El and Dan. Here too, the cleansers of Jerusalem's holy Temple burn those who profaned it by using the sacred site as a center for idolatry. **6:4–5. some of them they hanged upon a tree.** Esther 7:10 and 9:14 report that they hanged Haman and his ten sons upon the gallows that Haman had prepared for Mordechai and the rest of the Jews. I Maccabees also reports that the Syrian-Greeks hanged Jews for circumcising their sons. Thus, in both instances, the Jews turn the tables on the murderers, who were essentially hanged as a result of their own evil. As noted above, hanging may also imply a criminal sentence of strangulation. Strangulation would have been the punishment for kidnapping and selling someone into slavery. Greek society based itself upon slavery. Greek society denied freedom to a full one-third of its population. The Greeks were also guilty of perpetrating idolatry. In ancient Judea, an official convicted of leading others to idolatry would be sentenced to strangulation. **6:13–14. They would rebel against him and call him "the Fugitive."** According to II Maccabees 9:8–10, Antiochus falls suddenly and gravely ill with a divinely induced malady apparently meant to punish him measure for measure for the sins he committed and, at the same time, serve as a catalyst to repentance. He suffers agonizing pain as his flesh rots away. The stench of his decay repulsed all around him, even his own army. **6:15. threw himself into the sea.** This echoes Jonah 1:15, which depicts Jonah being thrown into the sea. In Jonah's case, however, his potential for repentance moves God to send a fish to rescue him. The fish swallows Jonah for three days, allowing him ample time to reflect. Jonah eventually does *t'shuvah* in the fish's belly and then acts as God's servant, bringing others to repent their ways and observe the tenets of God's morality. In the case of Antiochus, an arrogant mass murderer who attempts to remove God's influence from the world, no such potential for repentance exists. Even after the divinely induced malady alluded to above, designed to warn the king concerning his evil comportment, Antiochus persists in his immoral behaviors. II Maccabees 9:28 sees Antiochus being destroyed by his own evil: "Thus the murderer and blasphemer ended his life, with a most miserable death...after suffering the most terrible agonies, equal to those he had inflicted on others." I Maccabees 6:8–9 pictures Antiochus as killed by his own irrational hatred. When he hears news that the Maccabees had taken the Temple and were engaged in cleansing it, "he was astounded and badly shaken." He lies down for many days gripped by deep disappointment, and finally he dies.

6:16	Afterwards, the Hasmoneans came	אַחֲרֵי כֵן בָּאוּ בְּנֵי חַשְׁמוֹנַי
6:17	to the Temple and built the gates, and	לְבֵית הַמִּקְדָּשׁ, וַיִּבְנוּ הַשְּׁעָרִים,
6:18	closed up the breaches, and purified	וַיִּסְגְּרוּ הַפְּרָצוֹת, וַיְטַהֲרוּ אֶת
6:19	the court from the slain and from the	הָעֲזָרָה מִן הַהֲרוּגִים וּמִן
6:20	impurities. They sought pure olive oil	הַטֻּמְאוֹת. וַיְבַקְשׁוּ שֶׁמֶן זַיִת זָךְ
6:21	to kindle the menorah,	לְהַדְלִיק הַמְּנוֹרָה,
	but they found only	וְלֹא מָצְאוּ כִּי אִם
6:22	one bottle that had been sealed	צְלוֹחִית אַחַת אֲשֶׁר הָיְתָה חֲתוּמָה
6:23	with the seal of the High Priest so that	בְּטַבַּעַת הַכֹּהֵן הַגָּדוֹל,
6:24	they were sure of its purity, but there	וַיֵּדְעוּ כִּי הָיְתָה טְהוֹרָה, וְהָיָה
6:25	was only enough quantity to kindle for	בָהּ כְּשִׁעוּר הַדְלָקַת
6:26	one day. But God of the heavens,	יוֹם אֶחָד. וֵאלֹהֵי הַשָּׁמַיִם, אֲשֶׁר שִׁכֵּן
6:27	who caused God's name to dwell there,	שְׁמוֹ שָׁם,
6:28	gave a blessing, and they kindled from	נָתַן בְּרָכָה וְהִדְלִיקוּ מִמֶּנָּה
6:29	it eight days.	שְׁמוֹנָה יָמִים.

***P'shat*: 6:16. the Hasmoneans.** Mattathias and his sons, the Maccabees, were also known as the Hasmoneans. The family probably took its name from Mattathias's great-grandfather, Hasmoneus. **6:16–17. Afterwards, the Hasmoneans came to the Temple.** The purpose of the military battle was to gain the freedom to practice Judaism, an aspect of which concerned the cleansing of the Temple and the resumption of worship there. Having won the battle, the first place the victors go is the Temple in Jerusalem. **6:18. closed up the breaches.** The Syrian-Greeks not only desecrated the holiness of the Temple through the practice of idolatrous rites there, including sacrificing pigs and erecting a statue of Zeus, but they also destroyed parts of the building. **6:23. seal of the High Priest.** This seal would certify the quality and purity of the oil. Only the first drop extracted from each olive would be acceptable for illuminating the lamps of the menorah. In addition, the oil had to be guaranteed free from ritual impurity to be deemed appropriate to light the Temple's menorah. **6:24. sure of its purity.** The extent of Syrian-Greek wickedness may be discerned by the fact that they had purposely rendered the oil, vessels, altar, and the Temple itself ritually impure. **6:28–29. from it.** From the single bottle of oil, usually enough for only one day's kindling.

D'rash: 6:16–17. the Hasmoneans came to the Temple. I Maccabees 4:37–40 explains that when the Hasmoneans came to the Temple, they saw the sanctuary desolate, the altar profaned, and the gates burned. Bushes had sprung up in the Temple's courts, and the priests' chambers were in ruins. The Hasmoneans then tore their clothes, sprinkled themselves with ashes, mourned, and cried out to heaven. **6:17–18. built the gates, and closed up the breaches.** According to I Maccabees, they restored the gates and the priests' chambers and decorated the front of the Temple with golden crowns and small shields (4:57). Not knowing what to do about the altar that had been profaned, they decided to tear it down and store the stones in the precincts below the Temple. They then took unhewn stones and built a new altar like the former one (4:46–47). **6:18. closed up the breaches.** According to *Mishnah Midot* 2:3, they repaired the thirteen breaches that the Syrian-Greeks made in the *soreig*, the latticework surrounding the courtyard. Subsequently, the Rabbinic authorities decreed that when passing any of the repaired breaches, one should prostrate oneself in gratitude. **6:20–21. They sought pure olive oil to kindle the menorah.** According to Jonathan A. Goldstein, the act of kindling the menorah took place on the eve of the twenty-fifth of Kislev, inaugurating the rededication of the Temple. "It was an act which expressed the hope of a return of the *Shechinah* [God's Presence]."[2] This emphasis on the kindling may also account for the fact that Josephus knows the Festival of Dedication (Chanukah) by the name "Lights."[3] On the other hand, I Maccabees seems to regard the resumption of the sacrificial cult as the focal point of the rededication: "So they celebrated the dedication of the altar

[חֲנֻכַּת הַמִּזְבֵּחַ, *chanukat hamizbei-ach*] for eight days and joyfully offered burnt offerings; they offered a sacrifice of well-being and a thanksgiving offering" (4:56).
6:23. seal of the High Priest. The verse literally reads, the "ring" of the High Priest,
for he used a signet ring to apply his official seal. **6:23. seal of the High Priest.** The
seal assured the proper observance of the mitzvah of the oil as commanded in
Leviticus 24:2: "Command the Israelite people to bring you clear oil of beaten olives
for lighting, for kindling lamps regularly." **6:26. God of the heavens.** The same title of
God applied in relation to the military victory is now utilized concerning the miracle
of the oil. Thus, the midrash's inclusion of this title here implies that just as God
wrought the military victory over the Syrian-Greeks, so too does God cause the oil to
last for eight days.

6:30	Therefore, the Hasmoneans	עַל כֵּן
6:31	established an institution and made a	קִיְּמוּ בְנֵי חַשְׁמוֹנַי קִיּוּם,
6:32	prohibition,	וְחִזְּקוּ אִסָּר,
6:33	and the Children of Israel with them as one,	וּבְנֵי יִשְׂרָאֵל עִמָּהֶם כְּאֶחָד,
6:34	to make these eight days, days of feasting and rejoicing	לַעֲשׂוֹת שְׁמוֹנַת הַיָּמִים הָאֵלֶּה יְמֵי מִשְׁתֶּה
6:35	like the days of the Festivals that are	וְשִׂמְחָה כִּימֵי
6:36	written in the Torah, and to kindle	מוֹעֲדִים הַכְּתוּבִים
6:37	lamps on them to make known that	בַּתּוֹרָה, וּלְהַדְלִיק בָּהֶם נֵרוֹת
6:38	the God of the heavens had given	לְהוֹדִיעַ אֲשֶׁר עָשָׂה בָהֶם אֱלֹהֵי הַשָּׁמַיִם
6:39	them victories. And during them one	נִצּוּחִים. וּבָהֶם אֵין
6:40	may not give eulogy, nor may one	לִסְפֹּד וְלֹא
6:41	declare a fast, except for the	לִגְזֹר צוֹם, זוּלָתִי
6:42	individual's vow that must be	אֲשֶׁר יִהְיֶה עָלָיו נֶדֶר
6:43	discharged. But the Hasmoneans and	יְשַׁלְּמֶנּוּ, אַךְ חַשְׁמוֹנַי וּבָנָיו
6:44	their sons and their brothers did not	וַאֲחֵיהֶם לֹא גָזְרוּ בָהֶם
6:45	prohibit creative work or labor. And	לְבַטֵּל מְלָאכָה וַעֲבוֹדָה. וּמִן
6:46	from that time the Greek kingdom had	הָעֵת הַהִיא לֹא הָיָה
6:47	no renown.	שֵׁם לְמַלְכוּת יָוָן.

***P'shat*: 6:30. Therefore.** Because of the blessings of divine providence as evidenced by the Maccabees' victory against impossible odds, the people's return to their Temple and the worship therein, and the one-day supply of oil that burned for eight days. **6:31–32. made a prohibition.** They decree a ban on fasting and eulogies during the eight days of the festival, as these would interfere with the joyous mood of Chanukah. **6:34–36. feasting and rejoicing like the days of the Festivals that are written in the Torah.** While the aspects of joy and feasting might prove similar, the fact that the strict prohibitions on work associated with the biblical Festivals do not apply indicates that the days of Chanukah are not full holy days (see comment to 6:45 in the *d'rash* section). **6:44–45. did not prohibit creative work or labor.** As noted above, the strict prohibitions on creative work and labor apply only to those holy days established by the Torah. **6:46–47. the Greek kingdom had no renown.** Not only were the Syrian-Greeks (the Seleucid Empire) on the decline politically and militarily, for the age of Rome's dominance was beginning, but the lure of Hellenistic culture had apparently abated from among the Jewish masses. The Maccabees had saved the Jews from assimilation.

***D'rash*: 6:30–31. the Hasmoneans established an institution.** As per Josephus, their joy in rededicating the Temple after its violation by Antiochus was so great, for "they had unexpectedly regained the freedom of their worship," that they made it a law for their posterity that they should keep a festival "on account of the restoration of their Temple worship, for eight days" (*Antiquities* 12.8.7.324). **6:36–37. kindle lamps on them to make known.** This echoes Babylonian Talmud, *Shabbat* 23b, which speaks of kindling lamps in order to "publicize the miracle." Unlike the Talmud, however, which refers to publicizing the miracle of the oil, the midrash alludes to kindling lights to make known the victories that the God of the heavens had given the Jewish people. **6:41–42. except for the individual's vow.** The fact that individuals might still have vowed to fast during this period indicates that the observance of Chanukah during this early era may not have been universal. **6:45. creative work.** The Hebrew, מְלָאכָה (*m'lachah*), is a technical term indicating those specific acts that may not be performed on Shabbat or *Yom Tov* (a holy day). *Mishnah Shabbat* 7:2 lists thirty-nine such activities in relation to Shabbat: sowing, plowing, reaping, binding sheaves, threshing, winnowing, cleansing (sifting with a coarse sieve), grinding, sifting (with a fine sieve), kneading, baking, shearing or combing or dying wool, spinning, making two loops, weaving two threads, separating two threads, tying a knot or loosening one, sewing two stitches, tearing, hunting or slaughtering or flaying or salting an animal, or curing its skin or scraping it or cutting it up, writing two letters, erasing, building, demolishing, kindling, extinguishing, striking with a hammer (putting the finishing touches on an object), carrying an object from one domain to another. In the words of Rabbi Abraham Chill, *m'lachah* involves the "production, creation or transformation of an object."[4] All of the Shabbat prohibitions also apply to *Yom Tov* with the exception of those involving the preparation of food. One is permitted to prepare what one will eat that day. The above prohibitions apply only to those holy days officially established in the Torah. **6:46–47. the Greek kingdom had no renown.** Despite their power, wealth, technology, "high culture," military prowess, and sophistication, the Greeks would be lost from the stage of history. That is, the Greek civilization no longer exists, while Judaism shines into the future. The same may be said for the other empires that oppressed the Jews: the Egyptians, Babylonians, Assyrians, and Romans.

6:48	They accepted the rulership of the	וַיְקַבְּלוּ מַלְכוּת בְּנֵי
6:49	Hasmoneans, they and their children and	חַשְׁמוֹנַי, הֵם
6:50	their children's children, from that time	וּבְנֵיהֶם וּבְנֵי בְנֵיהֶם
6:51	until the destruction of the House of	מֵהָעֵת הַזֹּאת עַד חָרְבַּן
6:52	God, 206 years.	בֵּית הָאֱלֹהִים, מָאתַיִם וְשֵׁשׁ שָׁנִים,
6:53	Therefore, the Children of Israel	עַל כֵּן שׁוֹמְרִים בְּנֵי יִשְׂרָאֵל
6:54	observed these days in all their	הַיָּמִים הָאֵלֶּה בְּכָל
6:55	dispersion and called them days of	גָּלוּתָם, וַיִּקְרְאוּ לָהֶם יְמֵי
6:56	feasting and joy, from the twenty-fifth	מִשְׁתֶּה וְשִׂמְחָה, מֵחֲמִשָּׁה וְעֶשְׂרִים
6:57	of the month of Kislev, for eight days.	לְחֹדֶשׁ כִּסְלֵו שְׁמֹנָה יָמִים.
6:58	And the priests and the Levites and the	וְהַיָּמִים הָאֵלֶּה קִיְּמוּ וְקִבְּלוּ
6:59	Sages who were in the Temple	עֲלֵיהֶם וְעַל בְּנֵי בְנֵיהֶם עַד עוֹלָם
6:60	established and accepted these days	הַכֹּהֲנִים וְהַלְוִיִּם וְהַחֲכָמִים
6:61	upon themselves, and upon the children	אֲשֶׁר הָיוּ בְּבֵית הַמִּקְדָּשׁ,
6:62	of their children forever, that their seed	וְלֹא יָסוּרוּ מִזַּרְעָם
6:63	shall never neglect them.	עַד עוֹלָם.

***P'shat*: 6:48–49. They accepted the rulership of the Hasmoneans.** The Hasmoneans became kings of Judea and High Priests of the Jewish people. **6:49–50. they and their children and their children's children.** The Hasmoneans established a royal dynasty that stretched from 167 B.C.E. to 29 B.C.E. [5] **6:51–52. the destruction of the**

House of God. The Romans destroyed the Second Temple in the year 70 C.E. Its mention here reinforces the religious focus of the midrash. **6:53–55. the Children of Israel observed these days in all their dispersion.** During the Second Temple era, major Jewish communities existed in Babylonia and Egypt. **6:57. eight days.** The story of the oil that burned for eight days presented above (6:20–29) apparently set the length of the holiday, or at least punctuated the eight days of the Temple's rededication. **6:58–60. And the priests and the Levites and the Sages who were in the Temple established and accepted these days.** Just as the rebellion led by the Hasmoneans enjoyed popular support, so too did they not act alone in decreeing that these days of Chanukah be observed throughout the Jewish world from generation to generation.

D'rash: 6:51–52. the destruction of the House of God. The mention of the Temple's destruction here helps us to focus upon the Hasmoneans' true contribution to Judaism. Although the sovereignty that they inaugurated proved to be short-lived and the Temple was later destroyed, the battle against assimilation that they championed ensured the existence of Judaism to this day. **6:52. 206 years.** By even the most generous of calculations, the Hasmonean dynasty spanned only 140 years. The final descendant of the House of the Hasmoneans, Mariamne, wife of King Herod, died in 29 B.C.E., ninety-nine years before the destruction of the Second Temple in 70 C.E. However, the span of time between the consolidation of Jewish sovereignty (and of the Hasmonean dynasty) under Shimon's son John Hyrcanus in 135 B.C.E. until the destruction of the Second Temple does equal 206 years. **6:53–54. the Children of Israel observed these days in all their dispersion.** The Book of II Maccabees begins with a letter, dated 124 B.C.E., from the Jews of Jerusalem and the Land of Judea to the Jews of Egypt reminding them a second time to observe the festival of Chanukah. This would indicate that the observance of Chanukah may not have been universal in its incipient days. **6.53–55. The Children of Israel observed these days in all their dispersion.** Originally established in the Land of Israel, Chanukah, with its anti-assimilationist message, has remained an important religious practice throughout the Diaspora, where the powerful lure of foreign cultures and religions has sometimes been most keenly felt. **6:56–57. from the twenty-fifth of the month of Kislev.** According to I Maccabees 1:59, the Syrian-Greeks offered their first polluting sacrifice in the Temple upon the "abominating" altar that they had set up on the twenty-fifth of Kislev. The Temple's rededication then took place exactly three years to the day after that insidious event. **6:57. for eight days.** II Maccabees 10:6–7 presents the reason for the eight days of celebration as a reenactment of the festival of Sukkot (which biblically spans eight days, including Sh'mini Atzeret, the Eighth Day of Assembly), which the people were unable to observe, for they had been "wandering in the mountains and caves like wild animals" at its usual time, the fifteenth of Tishrei. In fact, II Maccabees refers to Chanukah as "the festival of Sukkot in the month of Kislev" (1:9). **6:58–60. And the priests and the Levites and the Sages who were in the Temple established and accepted these days.** According to II Maccabees 10:8, the authorities "decreed by public edict and ratified by a vote" to establish and accept and celebrate the days of Chanukah from year to year. The Talmud (*Shabbat* 23a) teaches that the Torah itself asserts the rights of the Rabbis to establish "commandments": "You shall appear before the levitical priests, or the magistrate in charge *at the time*...in accordance with the instructions given you and the ruling handed down to you; you must not deviate from the verdict that they announce to you either to the right or the left" (Deuteronomy 17:9, 11). Thus, the Rabbis prescribed that a blessing be uttered when kindling the Chanukah lights, "Blessed are You, Eternal our God, Sovereign of the universe, who hallows us with mitzvot and commands us to kindle the light of Chanukah," despite the postbiblical origin of the holiday. **6:60–63. established and accepted these days upon themselves, and upon the children of their children forever, that their seed shall never neglect them.** This parallels the conclusion of the Scroll of Esther: "The Jews established and accepted upon themselves and their children and all those who had joined them that they should not fail to observe these two days according to their writing and appointed time every year. Therefore, these days are to be remembered and kept throughout every generation, every family, every province, and every city; and these days of Purim shall never pass from the Jews, nor should the memory of them ever perish from their seed" (Esther 9:27–28).

On the Historicity of the Miracle of the Oil: A Brief Survey of Early Sources

According to the Talmud (*Shabbat* 23a), the event that originates and characterizes the celebration of Chanukah is the miracle of the single cruse of oil that burned for eight days. It is the answer to the famous Talmudic probe: מַאי חֲנוּכָּה? (*Mai Chanukah?*), "What is Chanukah?"

Jews have regarded the Talmud as authoritative for some fifteen hundred years. So naturally, this version of the events of Chanukah has dominated the Festival of Lights landscape. But in recent years, the story of the miracle of the oil has come under closer scholarly scrutiny, and many question the historicity of the events as reported by the Talmud. Arousing academic suspicions is the fact that the Talmud was finally edited in Babylonia no earlier than the year 500 C.E., more than 650 years after the events of the festival's origin in the Land of Israel; and those sources written closer in time and place to the events themselves, I Maccabees, II Maccabees, and Josephus, make no mention of the miracle. *M'gillat Antiochus*, which Rabbi Abraham Bloch argues to have been written toward the end of the first century C.E.,[6] while mentioning a one-day supply of oil that lasts for eight days, refers to the event as a "blessing," not a miracle. And even then, the midrash regards the lights as a device to "make known that the God of the heavens had given them [the Maccabees] victories" (6:37–39), not to commemorate the miracle of the oil.

In relating the events that led to the establishment of Chanukah, I Maccabees, written around 100 B.C.E. as an official court history for the House of the Hasmoneans,[7] according to Lawrence A. Schiffman, does make mention of the kindling of the menorah's lamps, but emphasizes the role of the Temple's altar in rededicating the holy place. The book depicts the priests' deliberations over what to do about the profaned altar, their tearing it down and storing the stones beneath the Temple Mount, and their building a new altar according to the Torah's specifications (I Maccabees 4:43–47). The book goes on to tell us that the priests then resumed the Temple's sacrificial cult, "celebrating the dedication of the altar for eight days, joyfully bringing burnt offerings; they sacrificed a peace offering and a thanksgiving offering" (I Maccabees 4:56). Jonathan A. Goldstein proposes the name of the holiday in the era of I Maccabees may well have been the Feast of the Dedication of the Altar or חֲנֻכַּת הַמִּזְבֵּחַ (*chanukat hamizbei-ach*), which eventually shortened to be known simply as Chanukah, "Dedication."[8] I Maccabees offers no explanation as to why the celebration lasts for eight days.

II Maccabees, which according to Jonathan A. Goldstein was written in the first century B.C.E. shortly after I Maccabees,[9] refers to Chanukah as the "Festival of Booths [סוכות, *Sukkot*] in the month of Kislev" (II Maccabees 1:9). Since the Torah prescribes the celebration of Sukkot for seven days and then, immediately afterwards, the observance of the Eighth Day of Assembly (שְׁמִינִי עֲצֶרֶת, Sh'mini Atzeret), the Maccabees' celebration of the purified Temple's rededication spanned eight days. The book mentions the "installing of lights" as part of the resumption of the life of the Temple, along with the building of a new altar, offering sacrifices, burning incense, and setting out the bread of display (II Maccabees 10:3). It also recounts how the Jews celebrated Sukkot as part of the rededication ceremonies, complete with palm branches and *Hallel* (psalms of praise) (10:6–7). II Maccabees makes no mention of an oil miracle connected with Chanukah. II Maccabees does, however, allude to a "festival of fire" associated with Nehemiah's dedication of the Second Temple (1:18) and to fire descending from heaven to ignite the wood of the altar when Moses dedicated the Tabernacle in the wilderness[10] and when Solomon dedicated the First Temple[11] (2:10). According to scholar Victor Tcherikover, II Maccabees' allusion to the above incidents implies that a similar miracle of fire occurred upon the rebuilt altar when the Hasmoneans purified and rededicated the Temple. These heavenly fires all concerned the altar, not the menorah.

Josephus, a native of the Land of Israel, published his *Jewish Antiquities* during the first century C.E.[12] He writes of the desolation of the Temple by Antiochus, the Maccabean victory, and the resumption of the Temple service, which included lighting the menorah, burning incense, placing the bread of display, and bringing sacrifices upon the new altar (12.8.6). He goes on to state that Y'hudah Maccabee celebrated "the festival of the restoration of the sacrifices of the Temple for eight days with the inclusion of sacrificial meat, hymns, and psalms" (12.8.7.323). According to Josephus, the Jews have observed this festival annually since the days of Y'hudah Maccabee through his (Josephus's) own day and call it "Lights." He conjectures as to the name: "I suppose the reason was because this liberty beyond our hopes appeared to us" (12.8.7.325). While Josephus's explanation of the festival's name seems rather cryptic, one can state with certainty that, like the other early sources, Josephus makes no mention of a miracle connected with the oil of the menorah.

M'gillat Taanit (מְגִלַּת תַּעֲנִית), an Aramaic document written during the Second Temple period,[13] lists thirty-five days celebrating various military victories upon which it is forbidden to fast or eulogize, the eight days of Chanukah among them. *M'gillat Taanit* does not, however, tell us anything about the menorah or the reason for the eight-day length of the festival. However, there exist three versions of the scholium, an ancient commentary on *M'gillat Taanit*, that relate various traditions concerning Chanukah. While the two versions of the scholium composed before the final editing of the Talmud do mention oil for the menorah, both of them emphasize the polluting of the Temple's vessels (including the menorah) by the Syrian-Greeks, not the lack of pure oil.[14] According to scholar Vered Noam, while the Babylonian Talmud constitutes the "sole source" for the episode of the oil that lasts for eight days, the early development of this story may be discerned from the "primitive form" found in the two early scholia.[15]

If Noam is correct and the legend of the miracle of the oil developed over time and became crystallized in its final form only in the Talmud, what considerations led the Rabbis to posit such a notion and to invest it with such importance?

Some argue that the Rabbis introduced the miracle of the oil to avert our focus from some other aspect of the Chanukah story: war and violence, animal sacrifice, and/ or the rule of the latter Hasmonean kings. Some opine that the Rabbis, weary from their own rash of military defeats and the oppression unleashed by the Romans in their aftermath, decided to concentrate upon the religious victory of the rededication of the Temple. After all, this religious victory spells the continual freedom of worship and Judaic practice that lasts into our own day. This enduring religious victory is symbolized by the eternal light of the menorah, not by the abrogated sacrificial cult or the short-lived political independence of the Hasmonean dynasty.

What's more, in one of history's great ironies, the latter Hasmonean kings became Hellenizers. They also flouted the laws of the Torah, as the Rabbis understand them, by serving as both king and High Priest simultaneously, and not being of the Zadokite priestly line from which the High Priest would traditionally be drawn. When the Pharisees (prototypes to the Rabbis) challenged Alexander Janneus on these points, he had 350 of them crucified. Therefore, the Rabbis may have used the story of the oil's miracle in an effort to maintain the religious focus of Chanukah and avoid glorifying the profligate Hasmonean dynasty.

Still others attribute Chanukah's origins to a pagan or folk festival. A festival of lights to brighten the shortest, darkest, and coldest days of the winter is a common cultural practice among many peoples. In fact, Josesphus's report that the people called this festival "Lights" without his being able to supply a plausible reason may attest to his attempting to gloss over the celebration's folk origins. Needing a definite religious reason to celebrate, perhaps the Rabbis chose to emphasize the single cruse of oil that shined for eight days.

Noam posits that the miracle of the oil serves to effectively explain why the holiday is celebrated for eight days. Attempts by the early sources to explain the eight-day duration by comparing the Maccabees' dedication of the Temple to the earlier dedications of Moses and Solomon seem vague. Solomon dedicated the First Temple for fourteen days (I Kings 8:65–66).[16] The princes brought gifts to dedicate the Tabernacle's[17] altar for twelve days (Numbers 7:1–89). II Maccabees' tie to Sukkot has no staying power, since it is once again possible to celebrate Sukkot in Tishrei and has for many years. An enduring Chanukah holiday needs its own identity. The miracle of the oil both provides that special identity for Chanukah, and leaves no doubt as to why the celebration should ensue for eight days.

The Rabbis understood well that there exist many brands of truth. There is historical truth, the realm of accurate and provable facts and figures. But religious truth also exists. Religious truth thrives on the attribution of meaning, the promulgation of concept, the understanding of the moral side of life, and the recognition of nuance. A story may well communicate profound religious truths regardless of historical accuracy.

For instance, the story of the Exodus from Egypt as related in the Book of Exodus does not stand upon faith in the historicity of the Ten Plagues as supernatural phenomena. Rather, the religious truths communicated by these "miracles" emerge as the vital points of the story and account for its lasting profundity. Specifically, the plagues communicate that God cares for God's people, that the Divine transcends nature, and that the Eternal champions human rights and values freedom and, therefore, so must we.

This same sense of religious truth may be evidenced in Chanukah and the story of the miracle of the oil. The Hebrew word for "miracle," *neis* (נֵס), literally refers to an ensign, banner, and/or a sign. Therefore, the one-day supply of oil that lasts for eight days elevates the following values so that they may be publicized and inform our behaviors: never giving up despite difficult odds; always take an active role in keeping our end of the covenant; God cares about religious freedom and so should we; if we keep our end, our Divine Covenantal Partner will ultimately support our right to live as Jews; despite hardships and obstacles, we can effect the spiritual splendor of redemption by who we are and what we do.

The symbol of the shining oil places the story of Chanukah on firm religious footing. The Festival of Dedication does not merely celebrate a military victory, political alliance, or territorial control. Rather, the Rabbinic focus upon the lights of the menorah reminds us that military victories come and go. Borders change. Politics shift. Even the Temple (and its altar) was destroyed in fewer than three hundred years subsequent to the events of Chanukah. But, the spirituality represented by the lights of the menorah yet shines in our present day and into the future. The menorah, or *ner tamid* (נֵר תָּמִיד), the continual light,[18] symbolizes the eternality of God and the Jewish people, and the constant vigilance that our mission to be a light unto the nations requires on our part. Despite the lure of the predominant culture and the "idolatries" of the day, defining ourselves by the tenets of Judaism and the distinctive lifestyle it demands brings not only survival, but fulfillment.

The miracle of the oil addresses the doubts that many may harbor concerning the victory of Judaism's survival against impossible odds. The story of the oil signals that our survival as Jews is no accident of nature, not the result of our superior numbers, or more effective military strategy, or more sophisticated technology, nor the chance of mere sociology. Rather, Jewish continuity is the result of our willingness as God's covenantal partners to take responsibility and action for divine purpose, and because God, loyal to the covenant, works "behind the scenes" to effect our survival. In other words, the miracle of the oil validates the miracle of the battle. It informs us that the Maccabee victory, our survival as Jews, our religious freedom, and our mission to be a light unto the nations are not the stuff of natural causes, but rather evidence of the hand of the Divine.

GLEANINGS

6:1 "The Children of Israel rejoiced"

Mixed Feelings

War is harsh and cruel, filled with blood and tears. While the joy of victory seized the whole people, among the community of fighters themselves there is a strange phenomenon: they cannot celebrate wholeheartedly. There is a large measure of sadness, of shock, mixed into their festivities. Some fighters cannot celebrate at all. The frontline soldiers saw with their own eyes—not only the glory of victory, but also its price—their fellow fighters fell at their sides in pools of blood. I know that the price paid by the enemy also touched a deep place in the hearts of many. Perhaps the Jewish people has never been educated and never become accustomed to the joy of the conqueror. Therefore, our victory is received with mixed feelings.

General Yitzchak Rabin, June 1967, quoted in
Noam Zion and David Dishon, *A Different Night:
The Family Participation Haggadah*, p. 101

6:14–15 "he threw himself into the sea"

Measure for Measure

In his [Antiochus's] arrogance he said, "When I get there I will make Jerusalem a cemetery of Jews." But the all-seeing Eternal, the God of Israel, struck him with an incurable and invisible blow. As soon as he stopped speaking, he was seized with a pain in his bowels, for which there was no relief, and with sharp internal tortures—and that very justly, for he had tortured the bowels of others with many and strange inflictions.

II Maccabees 9:4–6

6:28–29 "they kindled from it eight days"

Grooved Spits

Why are lamps kindled during Chanukah? Because when the sons of the Hasmoneans triumphed and enter the Temple, they found there eight spits of iron. They

91

grooved these out and kindled wicks in the oil they poured into the grooves.

P'sikta Rabbati 1:5

Lighting

Lighting tells us whether the actions in the story are clear and "well lit" or murky and mysterious. Much of what it means to become an adult is bound up in the ever-increasing light we experience. What originally was dimly understood and hardly controlled at all is later seen with clarity and often with some mastery.

Carol Ochs, *Our Lives as Torah*, p. 36

Menorah Miracle

The menorah reminds us of the miracle that no matter how dark life may be, there remains a source of light deep inside us. The light in our souls reflects and refracts the light from the One who is all brightness.

Michael Strassfeld, *The Jewish Holidays*, p. 177

The Miracle of Chanukah

By attacking the Torah the Greeks hit at the vitals of Jewish existence. They struck at the supernatural basis of Judaism. This necessitated a supernatural response. That response was the miracle of the festival of Hanukah, symbolized by the miracle of the oil, sufficient in quantity to burn one day, but burning eight days instead. The miracle of redemption, celebrated on Hanukah, is not the military victory of the Maccabees over the Greeks, but the miracle of the oil. A military victory only indicates the superiority of one physical force over another. True redemption, however, is grounded in spiritual victory over physical power.[19]

Byron L. Sherwin, *Mystical Theology and Social Dissent*, p. 151

6:61–62 *"upon the children of their children forever"*

Covenantal Continuity

The covenant extends throughout time to men, women, and children in every generation; to those born Jewish and to those who will become Jewish; to those who stood at Sinai and to those for whom Sinai is but a distant collective memory. It is a demanding idea, but an embracing one.

Rabbi Miriam Carey Berkowitz, in *The Women's Torah Commentary*, ed. Elyse Goldstein, p. 380

To Do Jewish

"How are we to be Jewish in this American society? The problem is not anti-Semitism; we're mainstream," he explains. "But we deserve the right to be ourselves. Still, we have to ask, 'What is it from the outside do I let in?'" ... At the mall one year, one of his sons asked, "Are all these people here Christmas people? But we're not Christmas people." The rabbi's reply? "We are Shabbat people." It was a good answer, he says in retrospect, because "the only way to 'do Jewish' is to do it regularly. You do it in the house, an inch a day, a little at a time—you get up the hill. You can't just have a strategy for November or December; the strategy needs to be year-round. You can't run, you can't hide—you need to make sure the Jewish pattern is the rhythm of the family."

Carin M. Smilk, quoting Rabbi Lance J. Sussman, in *Jewish Exponent* (Philadelphia), vol. 217, no. 12 (December 23, 2004), p. 14

Chanukah: A Rabbinic Response to the Forces of Assimilation

At first glance, *M'gillat Antiochus* may seem to present the Chanukah story as a mere history of military encounters between King Antiochus and the Jews of ancient Judea. A careful reading, however, reveals that the military confrontations serve as a metaphor for the true threat, that of assimilation. This is why the midrash mentions Alexander at the outset, for Alexander brought Greek culture to the ancient Near East.

Interestingly, the text contrasts Antiochus's intolerant behaviors with the ways of Alexander, his predecessor. But like the initial positive experience in Egypt that eventually led to bondage, so too may Antiochus's decrees outlawing Jewish practice be seen as an outgrowth of Alexander's introduction of Hellenism to the region.

Historical sources teach that the urge to assimilate into Greek culture proved incredibly strong among certain powerful Jews. In fact, when Antiochus intervened in Jewish life by means of decrees and military dispatch, he did so at the request of Jewish Hellenizers who wanted to eradicate the observance of the Sinaitic covenant and turn Jerusalem into a Greek-style *polis*. The challenge for the Jews then was not only political or military, but in actuality a culture clash.

Antiochus designed his decrees to bring about the demise of the Jewish people by causing their assimilation. The midrash emphasizes that the king chose to outlaw Shabbat, Rosh Chodesh, and circumcision because he deemed these Torah observances as essential to Jewish survival (as does the midrash's author). The Rabbis, therefore, stress their practice as a means to Jewish continuity.

Significantly, Shabbat, Rosh Chodesh, and circumcision may all be regarded as active pursuits. (Although some may conceive of Shabbat as refraining from work, the Rabbis interpret the commandment "Remember the Sabbath day to keep it holy" as a call to do those things that will make the day special.) This sense of action reflects the approach of the Maccabees to Jewish survival as depicted in *M'gillat Antiochus*. The Maccabees shape their Jewish destiny and pave the way for the Jewish future by their active opposition to Antiochus's decrees. The Pietists, on the other hand, adopt a passive approach to Jewish survival, symbolized by their hiding in a cave. The Pietists accept the rulership of Antiochus as a manifestation of God's will. They seclude themselves and wait for divine deliverance. Martyrdom, as opposed to fighting back, is their preferred response to the Syrian-Greek threat of death for Jewish observance.

Today we face an assimilationist threat every bit as real as that which confronted our ancestors in the days of Greek hegemony. Just as an attractive, "modern" Hellenistic culture lured our people in ancient days away from Jewish identity and the spiritual life of Judaism, so too do we today experience the attraction of a pervasive Christian-secular majority culture. The continuity of the mission of Israel and the survival of our individual Jewish souls amid this vast secular sea require that each of us make a conscious decision to swim against the tide, as it were. That is, regardless of pressures exerted by the majority culture, the continued performance of acts that champion the distinctiveness and beauty of Judaism spells continuity for our people and promotes the spiritual elevation of our souls.

The Maccabees, as depicted in *M'gillat Antiochus*, understood the importance of Judaism to our survival, both as a Jewish people with a mission to heal the world and to our fulfillment as Jewish individuals. They actively and courageously opposed those forces that sought to rob us of our heritage. The midrash communicates the need for us to do the same. We must bear the courage to take an active approach to invigorate our Jewish souls.

Chanukah, the Festival of Dedication, represents not only the Temple's rededication in ancient times, but our own rededication to what the Temple stood for—the covenant between the Jewish people and God, established at Sinai and extending into the future. For us to realize the spiritual promise of a Jewish future, we must actively shape our destinies through proud observance of the tenets of the covenant.

Where do we begin? *M'gillat Antiochus* teaches us that Shabbat, Rosh Chodesh, and circumcision prove to be indispensable to our spiritual continuity and Jewish identities. In the words of the great Reform rabbi Leo Baeck, "Without the Shabbat there is no Judaism."[1] Rosh Chodesh represents the Jewish calendar. The lexicon functions as the basis for culture and marks the festivals of the Jewish year, which are also known as מוֹעֲדִים (*mo-adim*). Although usually translated as "set times," *mo-adim* are literally "meeting places" between God and Israel, times of heightened spiritual focus and community gathering. Circumcision constitutes the ultimate indelible mark of Jewish identity. Significantly, all of these observances are mitzvot, commandments of the Torah.

Torah then is the vehicle that has sustained us as a spiritual people and carries the promise of a brighter future. The Maccabees fought to preserve Torah by adapting its observance to the needs of their generation. This sense of adaptation for the purpose of making the Torah vital and real in our daily lives is one of the essential concepts undergirding Reform Judaism. The Maccabean victory of Torah over the forces of assimilation shines as our victory as well.

The great symbol of this victory, the menorah (the seven-branched candelabrum of the Temple) is today represented by the *chanukiyah* (the nine-branched candelabrum of the Chanukah celebration). In the ancient life of the Temple, the menorah and its *ner tamid* (eternal light) represented not only the continuity of Temple worship, but the eternality of the Jewish people and their mission and of the God who commanded it. While the table bread of display represented God's physical sustenance, the lights of the menorah stood for divine spiritual blessing.

M'gillat Antiochus refers to the one-day supply of oil that lasts for eight days as a "blessing." Indeed, to exist only on the physical/material plane proves insufficient. We require a spiritual reason to be. We crave meaning in our lives. The midrash tells us that the victory of the Maccabees is not just military or political or entirely understood by the cleansing of the Temple and reconstituting the priestly cult there. Military triumphs may be short-lived. Political sovereignties may shift. Even the Temple does not stand forever, as the text so deftly points out. Rather, the importance of the Maccabee victory is that it preserved for all time the Jews' "reason to be" in the form of spiritual freedom. The lights of the menorah (and, by extension, the *chanukiyah*) symbolize that freedom.

The Book of Proverbs teaches, "The Torah is a lamp and the mitzvah a light" (Proverbs 6:23). The lights of Chanukah then may be thought of as the burning brightness of Torah and mitzvot communicating that Jewish spirituality is not some amorphous, romantic feeling, but a concrete program of action.

The Talmud instructs us to display the Chanukah lights in our doorways or our windows, where they may be shared with the world. This action informs the world of the divine blessing of spiritual and moral enlightenment that will lead to the messianic age, the time of universal peace and kindness. At the same time, placing our Chanukah lights in our windows is an arrant act of Jewish identity. It says that we take seriously our responsibility to be a "light unto the nations." It communicates to the world that we are proud to be counted among the Jewish people, because the Jewish people counts.

According to scholar Noam Zion, the *chanukiyah* in our windows symbolize our "light from within." That is, the Chanukah lights represent our courage in not allowing the outside world and its darkness to determine who we are and who we will be. Rather, our lights, and the psychological and spiritual strength they stand for, will have the power to brighten the world around us.[2]

We may be a numerical minority. Our values and religious practices may be disparate from those of the majority population. Historically, we may have had to struggle beneath the yoke of mighty empires. But we are still here walking in the "light of the Eternal," as the Bible envisions (Isaiah 2:5), while those supposedly great empires that had oppressed us have turned to dust. We are proud of the distinctiveness that makes us and keeps us Jews, for we have given much to the world and still have more to give. May our celebration of Chanukah manifest itself in our rededication to the Jewish spiritual path, the ways of righteousness and sanctity, the path of Torah, worship, and acts of loving-kindness.

Notes

The Historical Context of the Chanukah Story

1. Greenberg, *The Jewish Way: Living the Holidays*, p. 259.
2. That is, named after Antiochus IV. The members were known as citizens of Antioch in Jerusalem.

Toward an Understanding of Chanukah: The Role, History, and Structure of the Text

1. *National Jewish Population Survey of 2000-01*, Kotler-Berkowitz, Lawrence; Cohen, Steven M.; Ament, Jonathan; Klaff, Vivian; Mott, Frank; Peckerman-Neuman, Danyelle, principal authors, New York, New York: United Jewish Communities, 2002, p. 7.
2. I heard this in a lecture sponsored by the local Westchester Federation of Jewish Charities in 1995.
3. Although the Torah predates Chanukah and does not mention it specifically, the Rabbis have attempted to anachronistically read the Festival of Lights back into the Torah. For instance, Numbers 7:10–88 presents a lengthy list of gifts brought by each of the tribes to celebrate the dedication of the Tabernacle. Each tribe is represented, except the tribe of Levi, the tribe of the priests. The following section, Numbers 8:1–4, presents the priestly commandment of lighting the menorah. The midrash teaches that Scripture here alludes to Chanukah when the Maccabees (priests from the tribe of Levi) would dedicate the Temple through the mitzvah of kindling the menorah.
4. The other exclusive prayers are the Chanukah candle blessings; *HaNerot Halalu*, or "These Lamps," recited immediately after the lighting of the lamps to remind us of their holiness; and the medieval hymn "*Maoz Tzur*," or "Rock of Ages," usually sung as part of the lamp-lighting process. *Hallel*, while said on each day throughout Chanukah, is not exclusive to it. *Hallel* is also said on Pesach, Shavuot, Sukkot, and Rosh Chodesh.

5. These books were included in the Vulgate, the Latin translation of the Bible, and were preserved by the Catholic church.

6. Although the mentioning of the "oldest schools of Hillel and Shammai" could indicate material from before the Common Era, as Hillel and Shammai the elders lived in the first century B.C.E., the mention of the destruction of the Second Temple in our current version of *M'gillat Antiochus* precludes a date of publishing any earlier than the late first century C.E.

7. While this detail, along with those of prayer and forethought, are not indicated by the Book of Numbers, the midrashic tradition concerning Pinchas does mention them. See Babylonian Talmud, *Sanhedrin* 82a–b.

8. Goldstein, *I Maccabees*, Anchor Bible, p. 173.

9. Ibid.

10. Ibid.

11. Schiffman, *Understanding Second Temple and Rabbinic Judaism*, pp. 8–9.

12. I Maccabees 6:28–46.

13. I Maccabees 2:29–38; II Maccabees 6:11.

14. In addition, Yochanan introduces his prayer: "My God and God of my ancestors, Abraham, Isaac, and Jacob." This proves very reminiscent of the *Amidah*, the central Rabbinic prayer of the worship service, into which the *Al HaNisim* is inserted.

Chapter 1

1. *Gates of Prayer*, p. 45.

2. Rabbi Norman Cohen, Provost of Hebrew Union College–Jewish Institute of Religion, personal communication, 2003.

3. Tcherikover, *Hellenistic Civilization and the Jews*, pp. 30–31.

4. Crystal, "Source-Critical Analysis of *Ma'aseh Hanukkah*," p. 14.

5. Cited in Arnold and Silverstein, *Anti-Semitism: A Modern Perspective*, p. 32. For discussions concerning the scholarly evidence of the fraudulent nature of the *Protocols*, see Cohn, *Warrant for Genocide*, and Segel, *A Lie and a Libel*.

6. From an address given January 20, 1935. Cited by Joseph Baron, ed., in *A Treasury of Jewish Quotations* (Northvale, NJ: Jason Aronson, 1956), p. 427.

7. This statement is even included in Reform liturgy. See *Gates of Prayer*, p. 191.

8. *Theologico-Political Treatise*, chap. 3, cited in Baron, *A Treasury of Jewish Quotations*, p. 52.

9. According to Josephus, *Antiquities* 10.4, King Demetrius, who arrived from Rome, conquered Tripoli in Syria, and killed Antiochus V to assume the throne, sent

Nikanor and his forces into battle with Y'hudah Maccabee. Judah's army defeated that of Nikanor at Beit-Choron. Josephus lists Nikanor as the final casualty of that battle.

10. See *M'gillat Taanit*, mishnah 30.
11. Calloway, in *The New Oxford Annotated Apocrypha*, third edition (Coogan, Michael D., ed.), p. 205.
12. See Goldstein's commentary to *I Maccabees, Anchor Bible*, p. 142.
13. Bickerman, *From Ezra to the Last of the Maccabees*, p. 109.
14. Heschel, *The Sabbath*, pp. 3–10.
15. Rabbi Buchwald made this point in a 1991 recorded lecture entitled "Crash Course in Basic Judaism: The Sabbath," distributed by the New Jewish Outreach Program, in New York City.
16. Diamant, *New Jewish Baby Book*, p. 81.
17. Kushner, *The Book of Miracles*, p. 46.
18. From the blessing for the New Moon, recited out of doors upon viewing the moon during the first half of each Hebrew month as the image of the moon waxes. The worshipper, proclaiming the eternality of the Jewish people, thrice recites: "David, king of Israel, lives and endures." According to Philip Birnbaum (*Daily Prayerbook*, New York, NY: Hebrew Publishing Company, 1977, p. 563) the phrase alludes to Psalm 89:38 which assures that David's dynasty shall "like the moon be established forever." That is, the Jewish people may be compared to the moon in that it may wax and wane throughout history, but never completely fades from view. Interestingly, the Hebrew for the phrase, "David, king of Israel, lives and endures," דָּוִד מֶלֶךְ יִשְׂרָאֵל חַי וְקַיָּם, is identical to that of Rosh Chodesh (רֹאשׁ חוֹדֶשׁ).

Chapter 2

1. This is according to the opinion of Rabbi Moshe Feinstein. Some authorities, such as Rabbi A. H. Noeh, reduce this estimate by 10 percent, while others, like the Chazon Ish, increase it by about 10 percent. These opinions are cited in Carmell, *Aiding Talmud Study*, p. 77.
2. See also *Sh'mot Rabbah* 51:8, which regards the Torah as a sword to defeat the evil Inclination; and *B'reishit Rabbah* 21:9, which praises the swords of circumcision and Torah for their abilities to raise the human being from the "flaming fire" of *Geihinom*.
3. In Hoffman, *My People's Prayer Book*, vol. 3, *P'sukei D'Zimrah*, p. 140.

4. Stan Perlman pointed this out in a study session of the Etz Chaim Matmidim.

5. According to Rabbi Norman Cohen, it is "very possible" that the High Priest Chunya III and Yochanan the son of Mattathias are indeed the same person.

6. The Mishnah is divided into six orders or *s'darim* (סְדָרִים). The order entitled *Zeraim*, "Seeds," deals with agricultural matters.

7. In her commentary to I Maccabees 2:18, published in the *New Oxford Annotated Apocrypha*, p. 206.

8. The suggestion that Nikanor thought that palace security would protect him was made by Stan Perlman.

9. *The Encyclopedia of Jewish Religion* (New York: Holt, Rinehart and Winston, Inc., 1965), p. 299.

10. Leonard Smollen suggested that the mention of circumcision was rife with meaning because of Antiochus's decree, in a meeting of the Etz Chaim Matmidim.

11. See Numbers 19:14: "This is the ritual: When a person dies in a tent, whoever enters the tent and whoever is in the tent shall be impure seven days."

12. Zeitlin, *The Rise and Fall of the Judaean State*, p. 96.

13. See Genesis 9:4-7 and Genesis 2:16 from which the Rabbis derive these laws.

14. The term "light unto the nations" actually comes from Isaiah 49:6, "It is too light for you to be My servant, to establish the tribes of Jacob and to bring back the besieged of Israel, but I will make you a light unto the nations, so that My salvation shall be until the end of the earth."

15. See the ruling of Rav Chisda.

16. Nehama Leibowitz, *Studies in Bamidbar*, trans. Aryeh Newman (Jerusalem: World Zionist Organization), 1980, p. 331.

17. *Union Prayer Book* (New York: CCAR Press, 1940), p. 7.

Chapter 3

1. This ancient movement should not be confused with the modern movement of the same name. The latter movement was founded in Eastern Europe during the eighteenth century by the Baal Shem Tov.

2. By "modern North American Jewish movements," I mean Reform, Conservative, Orthodox, and Reconstructionist.

3. Hitler, *Mein Kampf*, pp. 316, 326.

4. Jerusalem Talmud, *Kiddushin* 1:7, based on Leviticus 12:3, "And on the eighth day *he* shall circumcise the flesh of his foreskin."

5. See Birnbaum, *Daily Prayer Book*, pp. 87, 88.

6. Babylonian Talmud, *Sanhedrin* 74a notes that violation of the prohibitions of murder, adultery and incest, and idolatry stands as exception to the rule, in that one should sacrifice one's life rather than transgressing them.

7. Goldstein, *I Maccabees*, Anchor Bible, p. 5.

8. Ibid., p. 235.

9. Schiffman, *Understanding Second Temple Rabbinic Judaism*, p. 385.

10. Tcherikover, *Hellenistic Civilization and the Jews*, pp. 196–7.

11. The word *rebbe* is Yiddish for "rabbi."

12. Although Ganzfried clarifies Isserles's gloss by adding more information to the story of the Chanukah victory wrought through the agency of a women, he alludes to the woman in question as "the daughter of the High Priest Yochanan." This is consonant with the tradition cited by the Ran (Rabbeinu Nisim) in his commentary to the Babylonian Talmud, *Shabbat* 23a.

13. This is according to Tel Aviv University Bible professor, Yehoshua M. Grintz. Linda Day, commentator for the *New Oxford Annotated Apocrypha*, more specifically opines authorship of the Book of Judith to have taken place during the rule of the Hasmonean dynasty (165–37 B.C.E.).

14. The ahistorical nature of the setting points to this conclusion. For instance, the story is set in the Second Temple period, yet depicts Nebuchadnezzar flourishing, despite the fact that he had already been long defeated by Cyrus. The book depicts him ruling over the Assyrians out of Nineveh, not over the Babylonians out of Babylon, as history teaches us. Not one mention of the town of Bethulia has been discovered anywhere else, leading one to conclude its fictitious nature. King Uzziah, depicted in the book, reigned during First Temple times, not second. In fact, Linda Day, commentator for the *New Oxford Annotated Apocrypha*, refers to the Book of Judith as "a well crafted work of fiction, an example of the ancient Jewish novel in the Greco-Roman period" (p. 32).

15. In fact, in *Maaseh Y'hudit*, a medieval minor midrash based upon the Book of Judith, Holofernes is called the king of Greece (as Antiochus is referred to in *M'gillat Antiochus*).

16. The text may be found in A. Jellinek's midrashic anthology, *Beit HaMidrash*. It also appears in Zion and Spectre, *A Different Light: The Hanukkah Book of Celebration*, pp. 42–43.

17. The *mikveh* is a ritual bath at which a woman purifies herself after her menstrual period. As the Torah forbids intercourse during menses and teaches that a woman can impart the spiritual impurity caused by menstrual blood to those whom she touches, immersion in the *mikveh* is seen as a prerequisite for marital relations.

18. This is an application of Leviticus 21:9, which states that a priest's daughter found guilty of adultery be sentenced to death and burned. The statement is a direct quote from the story of Judah and Tamar (Genesis 38:24), in which Judah falsely accuses his daughter-in-law Tamar of adultery, but finally admits, "She is more in the right than I" (Genesis 38:26). The line of King David begins with Tamar's progeny.

19. Cited in Eugene B. Borowitz, *Reform Judaism Today* (New York: Behrman House, 1983), p. xx.

20. Ibid., p. 31.

21. Rabbi Jill Hammer, "*Chag HaBanot:* The Festival of Daughters," Ritualwell.org.

Chapter 4

1. See *The Jewish Encyclopedia*, vol. 5, p. 105.

2. According to Jonathan A. Goldstein (*I Maccabees*, The Anchor Bible [New York: Doubleday, 1976]): "They spread open the scroll of the Torah at the passages where the gentiles sought to find analogies to their idols" (I Maccabees 3:48). In other words, the pagans had actually used the Torah in an attempt to justify their practices. The Maccabees then studied these particular passages to understand their true meanings.

3. The Nazirites were men or women who had taken upon themselves vows to serve God for a specified period of time by refraining from wine, strong drink, grape products, contact with the dead, and cutting their hair. Numbers 6:13–21 prescribes an elaborate sacrificial ritual to mark the completion of one's Nazirite vow. As sacrificial service could only be accomplished in the Temple, the Maccabees and their followers bewailed its desecration and occupation by the Syrian-Greeks.

4. The translation follows that appearing in *Gates of Repentance*, p. 139.

Chapter 5

1. Cited in Zion and Spectre, *A Different Light: The Hanukkah Book of Celebration*, p. 208.

2. Goldstein, *I Maccabees*, Anchor Bible, pp. 166, 169.

3. Lamm, *The Jewish Way in Death and Mourning*, p. 112.

4. *Romeo and Juliet* 11:2.

5. Rashi notes, as does the Talmud (*B'rachot* 13a), that the name "My Princess" implied that she owed her greatness to her status as Avraham's wife. She was a princess or governor to him, but not to others. "Princess" however, communicates the fact she had become a princess or "governor" to all the nations of the world, without any limiting qualifications. Sarah had arrived as the princess par excellence to all humankind.

6. Rosenblatt and Horwitz, *Wrestling with Angels*, p. 152.

7. To name only after the deceased is a custom of Ashkenazi Jewry. Sephardic Jews, on the other hand, do name after the living.

8. *Inside, Outside* is a novel written by Herman Wouk, published in 1985. In the quote that appears here, the author writes in the first person in the voice of the story's protagonist, I. David Goodkind.

Chapter 6

1. Nachmanides, in his comment to Deuteronomy 21:22, states that the court would hang in disgrace the body of a person executed by stoning for blasphemy or idolatry. II Kings 23:20 relates the burning of the bones of the idolatrous King Jeroboam as a consequence for his sins.

2. Goldstein, *I Maccabees*, Anchor Bible, p. 281.

3. See *Jewish Antiquities* 7.7.325.

4. Cited in Telushkin, *Jewish Literacy*, p. 599.

5. This is according to the calculations of scholar Elias Bickerman (*From Ezra to the Last of the Maccabees*, p. 185), who begins his count with the rulership of Mattathias during the rebellion against Antiochus and concludes his calculations with the death of Marianme, the wife of King Herod (whom the Romans placed in rulership).

6. See Bloch, *Biblical and Historical Background of the Jewish Holy Days*, pp. 64–66.

7. Schiffman, *Understanding Second Temple and Rabbinic Judaism*, p. 108.

8. The popular medieval Chanukah hymn "Maoz Tzur" (מָעֹז צוּר) features the phrase חֲנוּכַּת הַמִּזְבֵּחַ (*chanukat hamizbei-ach*), "dedication of the altar": "O mighty Rock of my salvation, to praise You is a delight. Restore my House of Prayer, and there we will bring a thanksgiving offering. When You will have prepared the slaughter for the blaspheming foe, then I shall complete with a song of praise the dedication of the altar."

9. In Goldstein's opinion, II Maccabees is an abridged version of the history of the Hasmonean era written by Jason of Cyrene as a "refutation of the dynastic propaganda" of I Maccabees. See *I Maccabees*, Anchor Bible, p. 175.

10. Leviticus 9:24.

11. II Chronicles 7:1.

12. See Schiffman, *Understanding Second Temple and Rabbinic Judaism*, p. 8.

13. See Noam, "The Miracle of the Cruse of Oil," p. 191.

14. Ibid., pp. 225–26.

15. Ibid.

16. Although the text delineates the dedication to have lasted "seven days and seven days, [totaling] fourteen days," Rashi explains that the first seven days preceded the festival of Sukkot (but included Yom Kippur, the Day of Atonement); the second seven days comprised the festival of Sukkot. The people then stayed one more day to celebrate Sh'mini Atzeret, the Eighth Day of Assembly. This second group of seven days, plus the one extra, of course, equals eight. Thus, some, including the scholia to *M'gillat Taanit*, allude to an eight-day period associated with Solomon's dedication of the First Temple.

17. The Tabernacle, or *Mishkan* (מִשְׁכָּן), was the Sanctuary the Children of Israel built in the wilderness after their liberation from Egypt.

18. *Ner tamid* has been translated in various ways: regular light, constant light, daily light, and/or eternal light. All of these terms reflect the fact that it was to burn on a continual basis each evening and, in order to keep it so, required the ongoing vigilance of the priests.

19. The author here is describing his understanding of the opinion of Rabbi Judah Loew of Prague, who lived during the sixteenth century C.E.. and wrote "Ner Mitzvah," a famous treatise on Chanukah.

Postscript

1. One of the most prominent German rabbis of the twentieth century, Leo Baeck, made this statement in an address on June 20, 1935; quoted in Baron, *A Treasury of Jewish Quotations*, p. 427.

2. I heard this from Professor Zion in a workshop held March 4, 2005, at Anshei Emeth Memorial Temple in New Brunswick, New Jersey.

Glossary

Alexander of Macedonia—Often referred to as Alexander the Great; he conquered Greece, Mesopotamia, and Egypt, including the kingdom of Judea in 332 B.C.E. He is responsible for introducing Greek culture to the ancient Middle East.

Al HaNisim—Literally, "For the Miracles"; the title and initial liturgical expression of one of the most prominent of the special Chanukah prayers. Worshipers insert the *Al HaNisim* into the daily and Shabbat *Amidah* and the *Birkat HaMazon* during Chanukah. *M'gillat Antiochus* reflects the flow and themes of the prayer. The Rabbis assigned another version of *Al HaNisim* to be used for Purim.

Amidah—The "Standing Prayer"; also known as *T'filah* (literally, "prayer"). It is the central Rabbinic text of the Jewish worship service. While the first three and the final three blessings remain constant, the middle section changes to accommodate the day. During weekdays the prayer includes thirteen blessings or requests. On Shabbat and/or holidays the middle section concerns the holiness of the day. The *Al HaNisim* is included in the section concerning thanksgiving throughout the eight days of Chanukah.

Antiochus IV—One of the thirteen Greek kings of the House of Seleucus who ruled Syria during the Hellenistic period, Antiochus IV, who dubbed himself "Epiphanes," or "god incarnate," reigned 175–163 B.C.E. His decrees forbidding the observance of Shabbat, Rosh Chodesh, and circumcision as well as his plundering and desecration of the Temple in Jerusalem galvanized the Jewish population of Judea to initiate the rebellion that led to the establishment of Chanukah. Antiochus IV appears in *M'gillat Antiochus* as the major villain of the midrash.

Apocrypha—Literally, "that which was left out"; non-canonical Jewish religious literature mostly written during the Second Temple period. These works were included in the Vulgate, the Latin translation of the Bible, and preserved by the Catholic church. The Apocrypha includes I and II Maccabees and the Book of Judith, all associated with Chanukah.

Bagris—Scholars consider the name to be a Hebraization of Bacchides, one of Antiochus's generals. Bagris appears in *M'gillat Antiochus* as the king's most important general and viceroy. His anti-Semitism and egotism rival the king's.

B'reishit Rabbah—Exegetic midrash on the Book of Genesis, stemming from the Land of Israel and probably written down sometime in the fourth century C.E., but containing earlier materials. *B'reishit Rabbah* is often quoted by Rashi and other classic commentators.

C.E.—An abbreviation denoting the Common Era. This designation is used for years since the year 0. This is the same period that is described by A.D. or *anno domini*, Latin for "year of our Lord," used in reference to years elapsed since the birth of Jesus. Since the notion of Jesus's deification is not consonant with Jewish theology, many Jews have adhered to the use of C.E.

chanukiyah—Although frequently referred to as a menorah, *chanukiyah* is the proper term for the Chanukah candelabrum. Although the *chanukiyah* is reminiscent of the menorah in design, the latter was exclusive to the Temple in Jerusalem and contained seven lamps, while the *chanukiyah* has nine lamps.

Chasidim—Not connected with the modern movement of the same name, in *M'gillat Antiochus* the Chasidim, or Pietists, practiced a form of Judaism so rigid that they chose to be martyred rather than defend themselves on the Sabbath. In general, they believed that King Antiochus ruled at divine behest and would therefore refuse to fight against him.

Halachot G'dolot—An early (eighth century C.E.) code of law written in Babylonia, arranged according to the tractates of the Talmud. Scholars consider its mention of *M'gillat Antiochus* to serve as an indication of the midrash's age.

Hallel—Literally, "Praise"; the name given to a rubric of the Jewish worship service offered on the biblically ordained festivals of Pesach, Shavuot, and Sukkot, on Rosh Chodesh, and on the postbiblical festival of Chanukah. *Hallel* consists of Psalms 113–118.

Hasmoneans—Also known as the Maccabees, the Hasmoneans were the priestly family of Mattathias and the dynasty founded by him. According to Josephus the name stems from Mattathias's great grandfather, Hasmoneus.

Hellenism—The mixture of Greek and Middle Eastern culture that initially swept the ancient Near East during the fourth century B.C.E. as a result of the conquest of Alexander of Macedonia. By the second century B.C.E., a large contingent of upper-class Jews in Jerusalem had assimilated into the ways of Hellenism, forsaking the covenant at Sinai. Antagonism between the Hellenists and traditional Jews contributed to Antiochus IV's attempt to suppress Judaism.

Isserles, Moses—A Polish rabbi who lived from 1525 to 1572, Isserles is famous for his glosses to Joseph Caro's *Shulchan Aruch* (The Set Table), which he called the *Mapa* (The Tablecloth). While Caro specified Sephardic practice in the *Shulchan Aruch*, Isserles cited Ashkenazic observances in his Mapa.

Josephus—A highly regarded historian, Flavius Josephus, also known by his Hebrew name Yosef ben Matityahu HaKohein, lived from approximately 38 to 100 C.E. during the era of Roman domination in the Land of Israel. Published in 93 C.E., his *Antiquities of the Jews*, a historical treatise spanning the history of the Jewish people from their beginnings to the outbreak of the war with Rome (66 C.E.), serves as one of the major sources of information concerning the Hellenistic era and the events that led to the establishment of Chanukah.

kashrut—Literally, "fitness"; the system of Jewish dietary laws. A combination of both biblical laws and Rabbinic expansions, kashrut has been practiced by Jews for thousands of years. Many consider its observance to be an essential element of Jewish identity and religious discipline and devotion.

Kiddush—The traditional prayer of sanctification, optimally recited over wine, a religious symbol of joy, on Sabbath and holidays. If no wine is available, the *Kiddush* may be recited over another beverage or even bread.

Maccabees—Otherwise known as the Hasmoneans, Maccabee was the additional name given to Mattathias and his five sons, the leaders of the Jewish rebellion against Antiochus IV, the Syrian-Greeks, and the Hellenizing Jews who sought to abolish the covenant established at Sinai. Many scholars debate the meaning and origin of the name Maccabee. Many opine that it means "hammer" and thus indicates military prowess. Others claim it to be an anagram of the biblical phrase of redemption from Exodus 15:11 that the Jewish fighters inscribed on their shields: "Who is like You, Eternal One, among the gods that are worshiped!" (מִי כָמֹכָה בָּאֵלִם יי, *Mi chamochah ba-eilim Adonai*). Although the majority of sources associate the name especially with

Mattathias's son Y'hudah, *M'gillat Antiochus* most associates the term "Maccabee" with Yochanan, his brother.

Maccabees, Books of the—The Apocrypha contains four books of the Maccabees. I and II Maccabees describe the events connected with the persecutions of Antiochus IV, the establishment of Chanukah, and the history of the Hasmonean family. Scholars estimate that I Maccabees was published during the reign of Alexander Janneus sometime around the year 90 B.C.E. II Maccabees was probably published a short time after, around the year 76 B.C.E. Pundits regard both I and II Maccabees as important historical documents concerning the Hellenistic era. *M'gillat Antiochus* shares many parallels with the first two books of the Maccabees.

Maimonides—Also known by the acronym Rambam, Maimonides was born in Spain in 1135. After leaving the country of his birth, Maimonides traveled to Palestine and eventually settled in Egypt, where he lived until his death in 1204. He wrote extensively on Jewish law and philosophy. He is best known for his code, the *Mishneh Torah*, the first section of which is *Sefer HaMitzvot*, a comprehensive list of all of the Torah's 613 commandments; and for his philosophic treatise, *Guide for the Perplexed*.

Mattathias—A priest who resided in the Judean town of Modi'in, Josesphus and I Macabees both credit Mattathias with starting the rebellion against Antiochus IV and his anti-Jewish edicts with an act of zealotry. When confronted with the abomination of an apostate Jew sacrificing a pig to a Greek god at a local altar, Mattathias rose up against the apostate and the Syrian-Greek officers who encouraged him. Mattathias's triumphant invitation, "Whoever is for the Eternal follow me!" won many Jews to his side of the conflict. Mattathias had five sons, who also became heroes of the rebellion: Y'hudah, Shimon, Yochanan, Yonatan, and Elazar.

M'chilta—An early exegetic midrash concerning most of the Book of Exodus, the M'chilta contains both halachic and aggadic materials; that is, both law and lore. Probably written down sometime in the fourth century C.E., the midrash contains tannaitic material and is also known as *M'chilta D'Rabbi Yishmael*.

menorah—A golden seven-branched candelabrum, the menorah was one of the most prominent features of the Tabernacle and, later, the First and Second Temples in Jerusalem. Exodus 25:31–40 commands the details of its construction. Exodus 27:21 lists the daily kindling of the lamps of the menorah as one of the priestly duties. The resumption, therefore, of its regular kindling served as a potent symbol of the rededication of the Temple and resumption of the priestly cult in the days of the Maccabees.

M'gillat Taanit—Literally, "Scroll of [the] Fast"; this Aramaic document, probably composed during the late Second Temple period, lists month by month the days of the Hebrew calendar that commemorate miraculous and/or celebratory events during which fasting is therefore prohibited. The scroll includes Chanukah and many of the military victories of the Maccabees. Scholars consider *M'gillat Taanit* and its scholia, Hebrew glosses that explain the reasons for the celebrations listed, to be valuable historical resources.

mid'oraita—Aramaic for "from the Torah," the Sages use this phrase to indicate the existence of a scriptural source for various Jewish laws. On the other hand, a rule that the bears the term *mid'rabanan* is of Rabbinic origin and therefore holds less weight than a mitzvah that is mentioned directly in the divine revelation of the Torah.

midrash—From the Hebrew verb *lidrosh*, to "extract" or "search out"; midrash is the class of Rabbinic literature that seeks to find contemporary meaning in biblical text by filling in between the lines of Scripture.

Mishnah—The compilation of Oral Torah explicating the laws of the Five Books of Moses, edited by Rabbi Y'hudah HaNasi in the year 200 C.E. The Mishnah and the Gemara, which helps explain the former, comprise the Talmud.

mitzvah—A divine commandment, a religious obligation; also used colloquially to indicate a good deed. Traditionally, the Rabbis regard the Torah as revealing 613 divine commandments, among them Shabbat, Rosh Chodesh, and circumcision.

Nikanor—A Syrian-Greek general who commanded Antiochus IV's forces against the Maccabees in 166–165 B.C.E. Historical sources indicate that Y'hudah Maccabee defeated and killed him Adar 13, 161 B.C.E. *M'gillat Taanit* teaches that this day be celebrated each year as "Nikanor Day." In *M'gillat Antiochus*, however, Yochanan, son of Mattathias, kills Nikanor while alone with him in the Temple, an act of righteous zealotry.

Pirkei Avot—Literally, "Chapters of the Ancestors"; the tractate of the Mishnah that deals exclusively with the tenets of ethical behavior as set down by the Sages from approximately the third century B.C.E. to the third century C.E.

polis—A Greek city-state. The *polis* inevitably included a gymnasium, Hellenistic school, a citizen's meeting hall, and other institutions reflecting a dedication to and a dissemination of Greek culture. Jewish citizens of the *polis*, by authority of King Antiochus, were officially exempt from Jewish law.

P'sikta Rabbati—A collection of forty-eight midrashic homilies for the Festivals and special Sabbaths of the year, compiled around the ninth century C.E.

Ran—Acronym for Rabbeinu Nisim, that is, Rabbi Nisim ben Reuven of Gerona in northern Spain. A famous fourteenth-century halachic authority (d. 1380 C.E.), the Ran is perhaps most noted for his commentary to Alfasi's work on the Talmud. The Ran is also known for a wealth of responsa literature.

Rashi—Acronym for Rabbi Shlomo Yitzchaki, medieval scholar (1040–1105 C.E.) who lived in Troyes, France. Rashi is famous for his authoritative commentaries to the Torah and Talmud.

Rosh Chodesh—Literally, "Head of the Month" or "New Moon," Rosh Chodesh in ancient days was celebrated as a minor holiday. The Sanhedrin, the high court in Jerusalem, had the authority to establish each new month upon the testimony of witnesses that the new moon had indeed appeared. The establishment of the New Moon is commanded by the Torah (Exodus 12:2) and serves as the basis of the Jewish calendar.

Saadyah Gaon—Born Saadyah ben Yosef, Saadyah left his native Egypt in 915 C.E. to settle in Babylonia, where he became the *gaon*, or leader, of the prestigious academy at Sura and, hence, a leader of world Jewry. Saadyah wrote extensively and even compiled his own siddur. His allusion to *M'gillat Antiochus* in his writings bears testimony to the age of the midrash.

Sanhedrin—A Hebraized Greek word, referring to the assembly of seventy-one ordained Sages that functioned as the court and legislature in Jerusalem. During the days of the Second Temple, the Sanhedrin met in the Chamber of Hewn Stone on the Temple Mount and held the authority to interpret Torah for the Jewish people and to proclaim the New Moon. Antiochus's decree against Shabbat, Rosh Chodesh, and circumcision (and the study of Torah, according to I Maccabees) therefore usurped their authority.

scholia—The Hebrew glosses that explain the reasons for the celebrations listed in *M'gillat Taanit*. Many believe that the scholia contain some of the earliest material regarding the "miracle of the oil," which reaches its final state of development in the Talmud.

Seleucus—One of Alexander's Greek generals, Seleucus ruled the area of Mesopotamia as king following the death of Alexander and the division of his empire in 323 B.C.E. King Antiochus IV, the protagonist of the Chanukah story, was a scion of the House of Seleucus.

Sforno—Popular appellation assigned to Rabbi Ovadyah ben Yaakov Sforno (1475–1550). Rabbi Ovadyah lived most of his life in Bologna, Italy, where he practiced medicine, conducted a yeshivah, and wrote classic commentaries to the Torah and *Pirkei Avot*. Sforno's commentaries generally seek to elucidate the *p'shat*, the plain meaning of the text.

Shulchan Aruch—Literally, "The Set Table," the *Shulchan Aruch* was written by Joseph Caro around the year 1560 C.E. Actually a condensed version of his *Bet Yosef*, a commentary on Jacob ben Asher's classic code, the *Arba Turim*, the *Shulchan Aruch* became a famous code in its own right, still held as authoritative by many Jews today. The code offers some insight into the celebration of Chanukah.

siddur—From the Hebrew word for "order," the siddur is the Jewish prayer book; in other words, the order of prayer.

Talmud—Vast collection of Rabbinic law and lore, consisting of two parts: the Mishnah, which seeks to interpret the Torah, and the Gemara, which seeks to "complete" the Mishnah by explaining what it really means. The Talmud appears in two versions: the more extensive "Babylonian Talmud," a collection of discussions by the Rabbis of Babylonia from the second to fifth centuries C.E., and the smaller "Jerusalem Talmud" (also known as the "Palestinian Talmud"), compiled by the Rabbis of the Land of Israel from the second to fourth centuries C.E.

Tanach—A term indicating the Hebrew Bible, *Tanach* (תַּנַ״ךְ), is an acronym derived from the first letters of the three sections of the Bible: Torah, the Five Books of Moses (תּוֹרָה); *N'vi-im*, Prophets (נְבִיאִים); and *K'tuvim*, Writings (כְּתוּבִים).

tikun olam—Literally, "healing the world"; refers to the activities involved in fixing those aspects of the world and society that constitute obstacles to the bringing of a messianic age to humankind.

Torah—Literally, "Teaching"; the Five Books of Moses, the first five books of the Bible, the sourcebook of Judaism. Traditionally, the Rabbis teach that the Five Books of Moses contain the 613 divinely revealed commandments that serve as the basis of

Jewish faith and behaviors. Sometimes the appellation is also used to describe the entire enterprise of Jewish holy learning.

t'shuvah—Frequently translated as "repentance," the Hebrew literally means "turning." As such, *t'shuvah* represents our turning away from sin and returning to God and to a higher vision of ourselves. The call to *t'shuvah* is one of the major themes of the High Holy Days, as the liturgy asserts, "*T'shuvah*, prayer, and *tzedakah* temper judgment's severe decree."

tzedakah—Literally, "righteousness"; the term often indicates our obligations to help others, particularly the poor.

Bibliography

Arnold, Caroline, and Silverstein, Herma. *Anti-Semitism: A Modern Perspective.* New York: Julian Messner, 1985.

Bayme, Steven. *Understanding Jewish History.* Jersey City, NJ: Ktav Publishing House, 1997.

Ben-Sasson, Hayim, ed. *A History of the Jewish People.* Cambridge, MA: Harvard University Press, 1985.

Bickerman, Elias. *From Ezra to the Last of the Maccabees.* New York: Schocken Books, 1947.

Bickerman, Elias. *The Jews in the Greek Age.* Cambridge, MA: Harvard University Press, 1988.

Bickerman, Elias. *The Maccabees.* New York: Schocken Books, 1947.

Bloch, Abraham. *The Biblical and Historical Background of the Jewish Holy Days.* New York: Ktav Publishing House, 1978.

Carmell, Aryeh. *Aiding Talmud Study.* Jerusalem: Feldheim Publishers, 1998.

Cohen, Norman J. *Voices From Genesis: Guiding Us through the Stages of Life.* Woodstock, VT: Jewish Lights Publishing, 1998.

Cohn, Norman. *Warrant for Genocide: The Jewish World Conspiracy and the Protocols of the Elders of Zion.* London: Serif Publishing, 1996.

Crystal, Darcy. "A Source-Critical Analysis of *Ma'aseh Hanukkah, Nusach Bet* and the Development of Hanukkah in Midrashic Tradition." Rabbinical thesis, Hebrew Union College–Jewish Institute of Religion, 2002.

Daily Prayer Book: Ha-Siddur Ha-Shalem. Edited by Philip Birnbaum. New York: Hebrew Publishing Company, 1949.

Diamant, Anita. *The New Jewish Baby Book: Names, Ceremonies, and Customs; A Guide for Today's Families.* 2nd ed. Woodstock, VT: Jewish Lights Publishing, 2005.

Encyclopedia of Jewish Religion. Edited by R.J. Zwi Werblowsky and Geoffrey Wigoder. New York: Holt, Rinehart and Winston, Inc., 1965.

Encyclopaedia Judaica. Edited by Cecil Roth. Jerusalem: Keter Publishing House, 1972.

Foxman, Abraham H. *Never Again? The Threat of the New Anti-Semitism.* New York: HarperCollins Publishers, 2003.

Frankel, Ellen. *The Five Books of Miriam: A Woman's Commentary on the Torah.* San Francisco: HarperSanFrancisco, 1998.

Gates of Prayer. Edited by Chaim Stern. New York: Central Conference of American Rabbis, 1975.

Gates of Repentance. Edited by Chaim Stern. New York: Central Conference of American Rabbis, 1978.

Gates of Shabbat: A Guide for Observing Shabbat. Edited by Mark Dov Shapiro. New York: Central Conference of American Rabbis, 1991.

Goldstein, Elyse, ed. *The Women's Torah Commentary.* Woodstock, VT: Jewish Lights Publishing, 2000.

Goldwurm, Hersh, Nosson Scherman, and Meir Zlotowitz. *Chanukah: Its History, Observance, and Significance.* Brooklyn: Mesorah Publications, 1981.

Goodman, Philip, ed. *The Hanukkah Anthology.* Philadelphia: Jewish Publication Society, 1992.

Greenberg, Irving, *The Jewish Way: Living the Holidays.* New York: Touchstone Publishing, 1988.

Heschel, Abraham Joshua. *The Sabbath: Its Meaning for Modern Man.* New York: Farrar, Straus and Giroux, 1951.

Hitler, Adolf. *Mein Kampf.* Translated by Ralph Manheim. Boston: Houghton Mifflin Company, 1971.

Hoffman, Lawrence, ed. *My People's Prayer Book: Traditional Prayers, Modern Commentaries*. Vol. 3, *P'sukei D'Zimrah*. Woodstock, VT: Jewish Lights Publishing, 1999.

Jaffe-Gill, Ellen, ed. *The Jewish Woman's Book of Wisdom: Thoughts from Prominent Jewish Women on Spirituality, Identity, Sisterhood, Family, and Faith*. Secaucus, NJ: Carol Publishing Group, 1998.

The Jewish Encyclopedia. Edited by Isidore Singer. New York: Funk and Wagnalls Company, 1904.

Jewish Exponent (Philadelphia) 217, no. 12 (December 23, 2004). Philadelphia.

Josephus, Flavius. *Antiquities*. In *The New Complete Works of Josephus*. Translated by William Whiston. Grand Rapids, MI: Kregel Publications, 1999.

Kitov, Eliyahu. *The Book of Our Heritage*. Translated by Nathan Bulman. Jerusalem: Feldheim Publishers, 1978.

Kushner, Lawrence. *The Book of Miracles*. New York: UAHC Press, 1987.

Lamm, Maurice. *The Jewish Way in Death and Mourning*. Middle Village, NY: Jonathan David Publishers, 1969.

I Maccabees: A New Translation. Translation and commentary by Jonathan A. Goldstein. The Anchor Bible. New York: Doubleday Publishing, 1976.

II Maccabees: A New Translation. Translation and commentary by Jonathan A. Goldstein. The Anchor Bible. New York: Doubleday Publishing, 1983.

Maimonides. *The Commandments: Sefer Ha-Mitzvot of Maimonides*. Translated by Charles B. Chavel. New York: Soncino Press, 1967.

Megillat Ta'anit. Edited by Ben-Tzion Luria. Jerusalem: Mosad Bialik, 1964.

New Oxford Annotated Apocrypha third edition. Edited by Michael D. Coogan. New York: Oxford University Press, 2001.

Noam, Vered. "The Miracle of the Cruse of Oil: The Metamorphosis of a Legend," *HUCA* 73, 2002.

Ochs, Carol. *Our Lives as Torah: Finding God in Our Own Stories*. San Francisco: Jossey-Bass, 2001.

Orenstein, Debra, ed. *Lifecycles. Vol. 1, Jewish Women on Life Passages and Personal Milestones.* Woodstock, VT: Jewish Lights Publishing, 1994.

Otzar Midrashim. Edited by J.D. Eisenstein. New York: Noble Offset Printers, 1915.

Partnow, Elaine Bernstein, ed. *The Quotable Jewish Woman.* Woodstock, VT: Jewish Lights Publishing, 2004.

Prager, Dennis and Joseph Telushkin. *Why the Jews? The Reason for Antisemitism.* New York: Simon & Schuster, 1983.

Rosenblatt, Naomi and Joshua Horwitz. *Wrestling with Angels: What Genesis Teaches Us about Our Spiritual Identity, Sexuality, and Personal Relationships.* New York: Dell Publishing, 1995.

Salkin, Jeffery K. *Searching for My Brothers: Jewish Men in a Gentile World.* New York: G. P. Putnam's Sons, 1999.

Schiffman, Lawrence H. *Understanding Second Temple and Rabbinic Judaism.* Edited by Jon Bloomberg and Samuel Kapustin. Jersey City: NJ: Ktav Publishing House, 2003.

Schwerd, Eliezer. *The Jewish Experience of Time.* Translated by Amnon Hadary. Northvale, NJ: Jason Aronson, 2000.

Segel, Binjamin W. *A Lie and a Libel: The History of the Protocols of the Elders of Zion.* Translated and edited by Richard S. Levy. Lincoln, NE: University of Nebraska Press, 1995.

Sherwin, Byron L. "*Mai Hanukkah:* What is Hanukkah?" In *CCAR Journal*, Fall 2003, pp. 19–28.

Sherwin, Byron L. *Mystical Theology and Social Dissent: The Life and Works of Judah Loew of Prague.* East Brunswick, NJ: Associated University Presses, 1982.

Stolper, Pinchas. *Living Beyond Time.* Brooklyn: Shaar Press, 2003.

Strassfeld, Michael. *A Book of Life.* New York: Schocken Books, 2002.

Strassfeld, Michael. *The Jewish Holidays: A Guide and Commentary.* New York: Harper & Row Publishers, 1985.

Tanenbaum, Leora, Claudia R. Chernov, and Hadassah Tropper. *Moonbeams: A Hadassah Rosh Hodesh Guide*. Edited by Carol Diament. Woodstock, VT: Jewish Lights Publishing, 2000.

Tcherikover, Victor. *Hellenistic Civilization and the Jews*. Philadelphia: Jewish Publication Society, 1959.

Telushkin, Joseph. *Jewish Literacy*. New York: William Morrow, 1991.

Telushkin, Joseph. *Jewish Wisdom: Ethical, Spiritual, and Historical Lessons from the Great Works and Thinkers*. New York: William Morrow, 1994.

Trepp, Leo. *The Complete Book of Jewish Observance*. New York: Behrman House and Simon and Schuster, 1980.

Wouk, Herman. *Inside, Outside*. Boston: Little, Brown, 1985.

Wylen, Stephen M. *The Jews in the Time of Jesus*. Mahwah, NJ: Paulist Press, 1996.

Zeitlin, Solomon. *The Rise and Fall of the Judaean State*. Philadelphia: Jewish Publication Society, 1962.

Zion, Noam, and Barbara Spectre. *A Different Light: The Hanukkah Book of Celebration*. New York: Devora Publishing, 2000.

Zion, Noam, and Barbara Spectre. *A Different Light: The Big Book of Hanukkah*. New York: Devora Publishing, 2000.

Zion, Noam & David Dishon. *A Different Night: The Family Participation Haggadah*. Jerusalem: Shalom Hartman Institute, 1997.

Zornberg, Avivah Gottlieb. *The Beginning of Desire: Reflections on Genesis*. New York: Doubleday, 1995.